Running on Faith

The Principles, Passion, and Pursuit of a Winning Life

Jason Lester

with Tim Vandehey

HarperOne
An Imprint of HarperCollinsPublishers

RUNNING ON FAITH: *The Principles, Passion, and Pursuit of a Winning Life.* Copyright © 2010 by Jason Lester. All rights reserved. Printed in the United States of America. No part of this book may be used or reproduced in any manner whatsoever without written permission except in the case of brief quotations embodied in critical articles and reviews. For information address HarperCollins Publishers, 10 East 53rd Street, New York, NY 10022.

HarperCollins books may be purchased for educational, business, or sales promotional use. For information please write: Special Markets Department, HarperCollins Publishers, 10 East 53rd Street, New York, NY 10022.

HarperCollins Web site: http://www.harpercollins.com

HarperCollins®, 📖 ®, and HarperOne™ are trademarks of HarperCollins Publishers

Ironman® is a registered trademark of World Triathlon Corporation

FIRST EDITION

Library of Congress Cataloging-in-Publication Data
Lester, Jason.
    Running on faith : the principles, passion, and pursuit of a
winning life / by Jason Lester, with Tim Vandehey.—1st ed.
        p.   cm.
    ISBN 978–0–06–196572–2
    1. Lester, Jason. 2. Lester, Jason—Religion. 3. Triathlon. 4. Ironman
triathlons. 5. Athletes—United States—Biography. 6. Athletes—
Religious life. 7. Athletes with disabilities—United States—
Biography. 8. Christian life. I. Vandehey, Tim. II. Title.
    GV697.L47A3   2010
    796.092—dc22
    [B]   2010007896

        10 11 12 13 14   OV/RRD   10 9 8 7 6 5 4 3 2 1

Contents

An Ultraman triathlon:

- Swim 6.2 miles
- Bike 261.4 miles
- Run 52.4 miles

People who finish Ironman triathlons each year: about 50,000

People who have finished an Ultraman triathlon: about 400

People who have finished the Ultraman World Championship and Ultraman Canada: 25

People who have finished both Ultraman Canada and the Ultraman World Championship in the same year: 15

Foreword

I first met Jason Lester via e-mail. I had known of him for a couple years as a challenged, Christian athlete who had been doing some impressive things. But after my book, *50/50*, came out in 2008, I got an e-mail from a guy out of the blue saying that he'd read the book and was inspired by it. I looked at the "From" line on the e-mail and it said, "Jason Lester." I thought, "Is this who I think it is?"

Challenged athletes like Jason have always been incredibly inspiring to me. When I think about what they have to overcome to compete in marathons, triathlons, ultramarathons, and other sports, it leaves me speechless and humbled, to say the least. When I was running in Wisconsin as part of my fifty marathons in fifty days adventure, a woman ran the course with me. She'd had her right leg amputated above the knee, but she told me that I had been an inspiration to her. Are you kidding me? This woman was out there on a prosthetic leg running sub-four-hour marathons. Her name was Amy Dodson, and she left a lasting impression on me.

When you see people with that kind of courage and commitment it absolutely shakes you to your core. It's awe-inspiring. When you've got the kind of body that can bang out one-hundred-mile races, it's easy to take it for granted. If

I used to, I don't anymore. Watching Jason and people like him has taken care of that.

So when I heard from him, I couldn't help but think, "Dude, you think I'm inspiring *you*?" For someone who's completely able-bodied and has all the athletic gifts, it's insane to participate in endurance sports and push your mind and body as far as you do. Competing in events like Badwater or Ultraman takes you to the brink of self-destruction. Just pushing yourself to finish something so punishing when every part of you is screaming to stop, lie down, and give in takes an effort of will that's superhuman.

Now, add a physical challenge like having only one leg or, in Jason's case, not being able to use your right arm. To gut through the normal mind-numbing violence of an ultra-endurance race while carrying the additional burden of not being able to use part of your body, and to not only finish, but excel . . . the word *inspirational* is somehow inadequate. It's unfathomable. It's unimaginable. But Jason and others do it.

Everyone in the triathlon world knows Jason since he won the ESPY for best male athlete with a disability. But he was well known before that, not just for his amazing performances in grueling races, but for his humility, his gratitude at being part of the Ironman® and Ultraman family, and his faith. I respect and admire Jason's faith and the fact that he has an open mind about himself and his sport. He's an explorer. He's not afraid to dig deeper, learn more, and find out just how far faith and discipline can take him.

In *Running on Faith,* you get to know Jason up close. I know him, and I know he's incredibly self-effacing about what he does—about how it's really not that unusual. Well, let me take a minute to set you straight. What Jason does is almost beyond belief. Imagine swimming two miles. Does that seem impossible? Now triple the distance and you have the swim that begins the Ultraman races. Think about having to swim that distance with your lungs burning and your shoulders screaming. Got a nice, clear mental picture? Good. Now, take away one arm.

Jason swims six miles in under six hours using only his left arm and his legs. That's so hard core it's difficult to even imagine. Now imagine that you've just reached the end of the swim, grateful to be back on dry land, and you've got to jump on a racing cycle and race for more than ninety miles. While the other competitors have been resting their legs and swimming mostly with their arms, you don't have that option. You've got to compensate for your immobile arm by kicking. So your quads and hamstrings are already fatigued by the time you get on the bike, but no one cares. They've all got their own agonies to deal with, big and small. You've got to deal or quit.

That's what Jason faces in every triathlon, especially every Ultraman. But he deals. He brings it. He trains with fierce intensity because he knows his legs have to hold up under that stress. He does it race after race. He never asks for special treatment from race officials because of his arm, and he never uses his challenge as an excuse for coming up short of his goals. He just says, "Let's get after it," over and over again. Even if you'll never run one hundred miles (or even one mile), you can appreciate that spirit.

When you make extreme-distance sports your life, it's like you have this angel sitting on your shoulder, constantly whispering, "Do something inconceivable. Set the bar higher. Take up a new challenge." Most days, you're too busy to listen, but when things quiet down you start asking yourself questions. *Could I improve my split? Could I set a new personal record? Could I keep going past the point where in the past I've quit?* It's about inner growth and improving discipline and mental focus. After all, the only person you ever really meet out on the course is yourself. You are your own ultimate competition; at the end of the day, you're the one you have to answer to.

One of my main sponsors is The North Face, whose tagline is "never stop exploring." That's Jason in a nutshell. His motto is "never stop," and he never does. He keeps training and competing when most triathletes have packed it in for the winter. Living in Hawaii helps, but what's more relevant is his extreme mentality. Like many extreme athletes, he's driven to create his own unique events. I understand that need perfectly, because I feel it, too. Athletes like me and Jason love to compete and we're motivated by competition, but we also love the purity of creating our own course and competing not against other athletes but against ourselves. That's when things get real. *How fast can I go this time? How much more can I do?*

That's why Jason created EPIC5, where he does five Ironman triathlons on five Hawaiian islands on five consecutive days. Most people hear that and think the guy's out of his mind. But he's not. He's an extreme, extreme athlete. For him, all his races, EPIC5 included, are about refusing to give in to any self-imposed limitations. When you have a physical challenge, it's easy to take the socially accepted path, listen to people telling you what you can't do, and sink into a self-pitying, woe-is-me mode. Not Jason. He's used his challenge to motivate himself to do things that are beyond the capabilities of most able-bodied people.

In this book, Jason talks a lot about something else that I understand very well: the shared warrior connection that extreme endurance athletes have with one another. Jason has said that Ironman and Ultraman have become his family, which might not make sense to someone who sees us trying to bury one another on the course in each race. It's true that there's competition, but there's also tremendous camaraderie between the athletes. When we're all together for an event, we're among like-minded people who share the same core values. Most important, each of us knows what the others have sacrificed and how hard they've worked. Passion, in these circles, is universal.

This shared disregard for limitations and stubborn unwillingness to allow anything to stand in the way of dreams creates a unique bond and special kinship among all athletes, able-bodied and challenged. It doesn't matter if you see one another only once a year at an event, or only read about your comrades' exploits in the magazines. They become your family, because you can relate firsthand to the toils they face and the struggles they must endure to cross the finish line. Respect is earned and deep mutual admiration garnered, no matter how fiercely you might compete out on the race course. They are your fellow warriors, your blood (and sweat and tears) brothers and sisters.

That connection doesn't just come into play before and after events, but during them. For example, I compete in the Western States Endurance Run, a one-hundred-mile trail marathon that attracts the top ultramarathoners from around the world. It's been said that in the Western States, you run against your competitors for the first fifty miles, and *with* them for the last fifty. I've seen some incredible acts of compassion from people I know to be ferocious competitors. When you see people at mile eighty-five throwing up on the side of the trail in lifeless heaps, you know the dues they've paid to get there. You want to pick them up and get them across the finish line, and I've seen competitors do exactly that.

I've been on the other end of it, too. I've been on my back by the side of the road when guys stopped to help me. I assumed they hated me because they were trying to beat me, but they came over to me and said, "You have to get across the finish line." And they sacrificed their own race performance to help me make it. That's a brotherhood beyond price. It's like what I've heard about soldiers who came home from war, having survived an experience no one else could imagine. When you've done that, you cling to the only other people who know what you've been through. They do become your family.

For the people who participate in them, extreme endurance sports are more than a compulsion, more than an obsession. The sports are an expression of who we are, a following of our deepest passions. Jason is no different. If you're not following your passions, you're not going to be fulfilled. Your interactions with others are not going to be as deep or meaningful as they might be otherwise. I think that if you're going to keep doing extreme endurance sports, you have to be that way, because the price we pay is enormous. Jason knows that. Jason made the sacrifices he needed to make to remain true to himself and to his faith.

Will and character are like muscles. To make a muscle grow, you push it to failure. That's what Jason has done with his whole life. His life is an extreme endurance race, and he's winning. Take a look at him today: he's at the pinnacle of his sport and he's only been doing it since 2006. Imagine what he could be doing in five years! But you can't separate the achievement from the sacrifice. He's sacrificed everything to get to this point. He's laid it all on the line with nothing to fall back on, and he's made it. I hear pro athletes in other sports talk about all they've sacrificed to be successful, but I doubt they know what real sacrifice is. Jason knows. There's no multimillion-dollar payday in what we do, no huge shoe deal or cologne line with our silhouette on it. What we do, we do for personal satisfaction and the thrill of pushing ourselves to a higher level of performance . . . and for the pure joy of exertion. You've got to be committed beyond a level most people can understand to sacrifice everything else in your life for that.

Inspire *him*? I don't think so. Jason Lester inspires me. He inspires me not to take for granted the physical gifts I have, to appreciate what I've been able to do, to cherish the endurance sport family that I'm part of, and to work to help other challenged athletes learn from his example that they can do anything. That will be Jason's legacy when his racing days are over: the death of the excuse. Can't get your butt out of bed to train? Bonked on the marathon and can't finish? Don't think you're good enough? Sorry, that doesn't wash, people will say. If Jason Lester did it with one good arm, then you can do it. Suck it up. Bring it. Keep pressing boldly onward.

To me, Jason's one of the people who represents the best in extreme endurance sports. His passion exudes from every pore. I'm honored to be part of his book. I'm proud to have him as a colleague and cocompetitor. But I'm even prouder to consider him a friend.

There may come a day when Jason Lester is no longer able to keep pushing himself to the extreme. But today is absolutely not that day. Go, brother Jason, go!

May you never stop . . .

—*Dean Karnazes*

Jason's Race Timeline

- April 15, 2007: Arizona Ironman (Jason's first Ironman)

- November 23–25, 2007: Ultraman World Championship in which Jason crewed for Mike Rouse

- December 4, 2007: Western Australia Ironman

- August 30–September 1, 2008: Ultraman Canada

- October 11, 2008: Ironman World Championship, Kailua-Kona, HI

- November 23–25, 2008: Ultraman World Championship, Kailua-Kona, HI

- May 30, 2009: Ironman 70.3 Hawaii (Honu 70.3)

- August 1–3, 2009: Ultraman Canada

- October 10, 2009: Ironman World Championship, Kailua-Kona, HI

- November 27–29, 2009: Ultraman World Championship, Kailua-Kona, HI

Introduction

Ironman World Championship 2009

"Endurance is not just the ability to bear a
hard thing, but to turn it into glory."

—William Barclay, Scottish theologian

The start of an Ironman®, the 2.4-mile swim, is absolute
madness.

My heart was pounding, my thoughts flying. Flashbacks
of 2008's blistering heat started running through my mind
like an enemy cackling *Gonna get you, sucker.* The Big Island
winds and heat can crush you. The doubts started. *I know I
trained for this, but was it enough? What about those sessions I
cut short or the days I trained too hard? Did I sleep enough? Did
I eat enough carbs this week?* The checklist started playing in
my head of things that could cause me to bonk—to run out
of the glycogen energy necessary to fuel my muscles.

I always situate myself about midpack at the start of the
swim. It's like a rugby scrum, like tsunami victims battling

to escape floodwaters, 1,600 bodies peeling out at the same time. On this particular morning I practically had my goggles knocked off and my face rearranged. Pull, tug, slam! *Why is the guy behind me pulling on my toes?*

I got past the bedlam near the start, but it was still chaotic with swimmers passing, jostling, and kicking me. It took about a mile, the first half of the race, for me to settle into a rhythm and find my stroke. The ocean was calm and I felt great. All I was thinking was if I kept this pace I would have a great, strong swim. Based on my previous Ironman swims I knew I would finish in about 1:30 to 1:35, depending on the water conditions, but that day I thought I might even set a PR, a personal record.

When I'm swimming in a race, it's hard to tell how fast I'm going. I have to look at the other competitors to see their swim technique—that's how I recognize a good swimmer. That day I was keeping up with the solid swimmers. In previous races I had gone out hard in order to find a good position, but this time I was swimming effortlessly. I wasn't even gasping to catch my breath! I kicked back, relaxed, and tried to remember that I still had a long day ahead of me. I hit the turn buoy, headed back toward the pier, and got out of the water in 1:27—a PR of ten minutes off my previous time! But I knew the hardest work was still in front of me. After some cooler and cloudy days, the morning had turned into the worst kind of day for a triathlon: hot.

I got to the transition area, the place where athletes shed the gear from one stage and gear up for another. As I ran up to the changing tent with my gear bag I heard someone shout, "Jason, over here!" I looked up, and it was my friends

Dave and Andrew, triathletes who were volunteering this year. I sat down, and they stripped my speed suit off and had my bike shoes, socks, arm brace, helmet, and glasses on me in less than four minutes. Then I was out of the tent and off to the bike racks to grab my bike. Walking from the bike rack to the line where you can mount your bike always seems to take forever. Transition time counts against your total race time, so a fast transition is crucial.

When I got on the bike, I felt great. For the first thirty-plus miles out to the town of Kawaihae I was strong and confident. From there, the course would take us up to the sleepy town of Hawi (pronounced ha-VEE), where we would turn around and head back to Kailua-Kona. The climb to Hawi is hot and at times windy; we had our work cut out for us. It's a gradual climb that we would definitely feel in the blistering heat.

When I got to the turnaround the timer said 4:38, and by subtracting fifteen minutes because that clock starts when the pros start their race, I was at 4:23. *Awesome,* I thought. *I might finish in eleven hours.* That would be a monster improvement over last year's Ironman. I made the turn, grabbed my special needs bag, loaded up my new fuel bottles, and felt stoked that I had an eighteen-mile downhill ride and was headed home.

Bam! A vicious crosswind slammed into me. Strong winds are common on the northwest side of the Big Island, and there's not a cyclist who doesn't hate them. So I was trying to hold on to my bike and stay up with one arm, which took energy I didn't really have to spare. Plus I weighed only 138 pounds in this race, nine pounds down from my Ultraman race weight just two and a half months prior, so I was blown around a lot for the next fifteen miles. Finishing in less than twelve hours? Man, I was just hoping to stay in one piece.

Then things got even tougher: I got back down to Queen Ka'ahumanu Highway and ran right into a headwind. All I could think was *Okay, this sucks.* The only thing I could do was put my head down for the next three hours and grind. I couldn't take my good arm off the bike in the strong wind long enough to reach for my water, so I was cycling in a wind tunnel, the temperature was about a hundred degrees, and I couldn't drink. The one time I did try to sneak my arm down and grab my water, the wind almost knocked me to the other side of the island and scared the daylights out of me and the nearby athletes. *Screw it,* I thought. *I'll drink later.* Then I realized that if I didn't drink on the course, I would blow up and bonk. So after about mile seventy, I started to pull over at every other aid station to reload my bottle and stay hydrated.

It became all about finishing the race. I was overheating and dumping bottle after bottle of water over my head. Starting about six miles out, near Kona International Airport, I knew the marathon was going to be hell. The pros were starting to run out of energy. I could tell by looking at how wet they were and all the salt that had accumulated on their shorts that they were suffering. I could smell the finish of this long 112-mile bike ride, and I was happy to be out of the saddle and onto the third and final leg of this mission. I dismounted at the finish line, grabbed my transition bag, and headed into the changing tent. The temperature felt like 150 as I sat with fifty other overheated men, each of us dreading the coming twenty-six-mile run. Helmet and shoes flew off, and on came my running shoes and fuel belt. The fluids in my bottles must have been boiling.

In the first mile of the run, it felt like my face was pulsating with the heat. I slowed down, but I was still boiling over. I was dumping cupfuls of ice down my back, shorts, and chest, but it wasn't helping much. This is where the volunteers really came through. When the Ironman becomes a marathon, it becomes a much more intimate race. It's at street level, you can see the athletes' faces, and you connect with the ones you know. The great thing is it doesn't matter whether you know them or not; everyone is out cheering for everyone else. As I ran down Ali'i Drive, the waterfront road in Kailua-Kona, I could hear person after person cheering me on. It was overwhelming at times; I felt blessed. I could hear "Go, Lester!" echo from the crowd for the next four hours. It's what pushed me to run the next mile, to the next aid station, and to the next fan, friend, or family I hoped would inspire me to keep going.

As I hit mile marker five, my coach, Dave Ciaverella, jumped out in the street to cheer me on. "Jason, you look great, keep it up." *I look great? I feel like an overheated engine in the Mojave Desert. Please, please stop telling me I look great!* We hit mile six, and it was time to backtrack up Ali'i Drive. Dave was there again at mile seven, and he screamed, "Jason, look at me, Jason—listen. When you hit mile sixteen, I want you to pound it and hammer hard!"

Hammer hard? I'm trying to figure out how I can get my temperature under 150 degrees, and he's telling me to hammer it? *One foot in front of the other* was all I was thinking. *Drink as much as you can, ice down at every aid station, and continue to pray for strength.*

5

I got about two miles out of town, and there was Dave again. All I could focus on was how much ice I could hold in my shorts. I couldn't wait to see the next aid station, but when I arrived they had run out of cups of ice and had only softball-size ice cubes to cool the water. *I'll take one of those please.* Dunk—right into the shorts. It was big and cold, but it helped cool my core. Thank God. Not long after that, I ran into a group of what must have been a hundred people shouting, "Let's go, Kona boy, let's go, Lester!" Right then I knew that I couldn't let anybody down. I wasn't going to stop.

You're not letting these people down, I told myself. Before I knew it, there was my coach again, saying, "Jason, when you get to mile sixteen, I want you to lay it all on the line." *Sure, Dave.* I had nothing to lay on the line. But at mile sixteen I started drinking soda and water, then started to feel the quick shot of glucose. It gave me a rush of new life. I started pounding a half cup of Coke chased with a half cup of water at every aid station. Then the sun started to go down a bit as I turned around to head back up to the Queen Ka'ahumanu Highway. *Hallelujah.* I felt myself starting to pick it up. Each stride was longer, I was breathing with less effort, and I was feeling like a fresh runner. I was running with a smile, my core temperature dropped, and I was off to the finish line.

Then all of a sudden I was overwhelmed with tears. I was having flashbacks. Flashbacks of my life, my childhood, and my father who never saw me run, let alone race. I started to feel pain, not in my lungs or my legs but in my heart. It hit me. His last memories of me were of a twelve-year-old boy lying in the intensive care unit with casts on every limb but my limp right arm. Why was I having these emotions? I was about to finish the 2009 Ironman World Championship at right around twelve hours. Why now?

Dad, are you there? Are you with me? Strangely, I felt like I was floating. I knew he *was* there—my earthly father and my heavenly father were there with me as they always have been. I ran my final miles thinking of how amazing God was to take a boy who lost his mother, his father—everything—and give him the whole world.

When you're racing and you see the lights of Kona in the distance, it's incredibly beautiful, like seeing land when you're lost at sea. I came down toward Ironman central, and I could hear the announcer saying the names and hometowns of people as they crossed the finish line, and that started fueling me.

There's nothing like the finish chute of an Ironman. The race becomes even more intimate down that last stretch. The finish along Ali'i Drive runs along a narrow street lined with shops, bars, and restaurants on one side and a beach on the other. There are balloons, banners, and inflatable archways all leading to that miraculous finish line ramp and time clock. When you're coming down the final half mile, the entire route is lined with screaming fans, some of whom stay out there until the last competitors straggle in at midnight. What really makes it wonderful is that they're shouting for every athlete whether they know them or not.

When I banked right to Ali'i Drive toward the finish line, something really special happened. A guy I know, whose six-year-old grandson Christian swims on the local team, yells to me, "He's going to run with you!" Out runs this kid; Christian fell into pace with me as I ran along Ali'i, past fans screaming and high-fiving me. All the way, this kid was repeating, "Let's pick it up!" I reached down to give him a low five, and he screamed over the crowd, "You're the best in the world! You're a winner! Faster, faster!"

It was awesome. I was exhausted and in pain and in tears, and it was one of the most unforgettable runs of my life. It was as if God sent me a little angel to run those final yards. God knows our pains and our hurts, and he never forsakes us. I have a little five-year-old daughter who has never seen her daddy race, but little Christian, who is around the same age, was sent to run to the finish line with me on my special day. Prayer answered.

We all suffer when we do Ironman, but it's a joyful agony. As I approached the finish line I could hear announcer Mike Reilly scream, "And from right here in Kailua-Kona, Hawaii, your very own Jason Lester!" I blew a huge kiss to the sky and said to God, "This is all for you!" I crossed the finish to massive hometown cheers, and I ended up with a negative split in the second half of the marathon, meaning I ran the second half faster than the first. That's the power of God, love, and Coca-Cola.

I think it's that spirit of universal support that makes the Ironman World Championship in Kona so special. You have a city full of people whose main reason for being there is to show love and support for the people running the race without caring who they are, where they're from, or how fast they're going. It's like the fans are cheering because a fellow member of the human race is doing this marvelous, impossible thing that elevates all of us. I think the unconditional love we, the athletes, feel from the fans is as inspiring as doing the Ironman itself. It's people at their absolute finest.

The real drama near the finish comes from the faces of the competitors. The pros are long since resting and doing interviews when the athletes who have been out for thirteen or fourteen hours or more come down the chute. Their expressions are almost poetic. They tend to fall into three categories. First is the exultant runner who's dreamed about this his or her entire life, is doing pretty well, and comes down the last few hundred yards smiling, waving, and high-fiving the fans. A few even raise their arms to call for some whoop-whoop from the crowd. There's pure, unfiltered joy in their eyes. It's beautiful.

Then there are the ones who are in the zone. They don't look to the side. They don't smile. They may not even know the fans are there. They're in pain, and all their will is focused on getting their legs over the finish line. Finally, there are the ones who are hurting. They might be walking, or they might be running at a crawl, listing to one side, nearly collapsing from exhaustion, nursing a hamstring or calf injury, dehydrated, and barely hanging on. More than a few of the older or less experienced competitors cross the finish line with a medic at their sides and head straight for the medical tent for IV fluids.

But it doesn't matter. To triathletes and our fans, only one thing matters: you're out there, you're giving it your all, and you finish. It doesn't matter if you finish walking (as a lot of late finishers do) at sixteen hours and fifty-nine minutes. It's not the speed that makes people cheer and scream for strangers and work all day in the hot sun. It's the sacrifice and hard work and determination not to give up. Ironman may as well be called Inspirationman.

There are Ironman races, triathlons that go the official Ironman distance, and then there's *the* Ironman, the original Ironman, the iconic race in Kailua-Kona, on the Big Island of Hawaii, which tens of thousands of athletes aspire to be part of each year. To a dedicated triathlete, the word *Ironman* means only one thing: the Ironman World Championship. Like making a pilgrimage to Mecca for a Muslim or climbing Everest for a mountaineer, it's the defining moment of many people's lives, what they work for years to achieve.

For about one hundred and sixty professional triathletes,* the Ironman World Championship is like the Masters for golfers: the peak event of their season, the chance for a nice financial payoff and to make sponsors very, very happy. But to me, the Ironman is something else even bigger: an exhibition of human beings at our absolute best, as God intended us to be.

Start with the athletes. The 2009 Ironman featured a man who was competing three years to the day after he received a new heart, and Rudy Garcia-Tolson, a double amputee who had been born with webbed legs, who had to propel

---

*Pros differ from the rest of us who compete in the age groups in several ways. They typically have big-name sponsors, so they can afford to hire top coaches, nutritionists, and others to help them optimize their training. They earn most of their income from races and sponsorships, unlike most "age groupers," who work regular jobs. And pros all compete against one another, regardless of age. They're the elite of Ironman, the men and women who often finish in under nine hours.

his specially designed bike in the cycling stage of the race *without having quadriceps,* pumping his prosthetics using only his glutes. There was David Bailey, a paraplegic who completed the swim in only 1:24. There were 41 athletes over seventy years old and more than 500 competitors over age fifty. Of the nearly 1,800 people who started the day, 92.9 percent finished the race in under the total cutoff time of seventeen hours.

There were athletes from fifty-seven countries and five continents: Germany, Japan, Argentina, Australia, Canada, the United Kingdom, and more, every one of them with his or her own story. Some have beaten cancer or heart disease diagnoses. Others have lost massive amounts of weight. Others are recovering from injuries or trying to restart their lives after a divorce. Many are just trying to prove something to themselves, to do something extraordinary. When Ironman pulls into town, the west coast of the Big Island is overflowing with incredible stories of loss, courage, and determination. Mine is just one of them.

• • •

The Ironman World Championship is the big event of the year in Kailua-Kona (Kona, as the locals call it), the otherwise sleepy town that I've made my home. When the race comes to town, everything else shuts down. Up to 1,800 athletes, thousands of crew and support team members, thousands more volunteers, and tens of thousands of tourists descend on Kona, occupying every hotel room and driving rental car rates through the roof. The streets are infected with Ironman fever; half the businesses in the town have

WELCOME, TRIATHLETES signs on their front windows. Here and there you find Ironman groupies who can't get enough of anything involving triathlons in general and Ironman in particular. They are some of the most hard-core fans around, and they make great race volunteers.

Into this party atmosphere in 2009 came nearly two thousand of the fittest people on earth, including Chrissie Wellington, the two-time (now three-time) Ironman winner who was expected to dominate the race among the women. The intersection of Palani Way and Ali'i Drive, on the Kona waterfront, transformed into Ironman central, with the action focused on the Kailua-Kona Pier, where the swim starts and ends and the athletes transition from one stage to another. All around, streets were closed, barriers and cones turned other roads into lanes for cyclists and runners, and corporate sponsor banners could be seen everywhere. At the "hot corner" where the cycling stage would end and the marathon would begin was a media tower for the race announcer and the TV cameras. Thousands of fans would converge on that intersection later in the day to scream for their favorite athletes.

Around the world, hundreds of triathlons are run each year, with twenty-four Ironman qualifying races—races of the traditional Ironman length of a 2.4-mile swim, 112-mile bike ride, and 26.2-mile run—that qualify those who place for the most prestigious race of all, the Ironman World Championship in Kona. It's the original Ironman race, tracing its roots to 1977 on the Hawaiian island of Oahu, when U.S. Navy commander John Collins suggested to a group of distance runners that they settle the debate over who was the fittest—runners, swimmers, or cyclists—by creating a triathlon that combined three extreme races already being held on Oahu: the Waikiki Roughwater Swim (2.4 miles), the Around-Oahu Bike Race (115 miles), and the Honolulu Marathon. Whoever finished first would earn the title Ironman.

Fifteen men ran in that first Ironman, including a Navy SEAL named John Dunbar, who ran out of water during the marathon and drank beer instead. With that grueling race, a legend was born. People had a new way to test themselves against their own limits—something humans have always loved doing. Today the triathlon is an Olympic sport, and the Ironman and other extreme races like the Ultraman (a double-length Ironman, which only the truly hard core will even try) are international phenomena. From the Leadville 100 trail run to the lethal Badwater ultramarathon through the 125-degree heat of Death Valley, opportunities abound for indulging our fascination with finding out just how far we can push the human body. Only a few exceptional athletes can even complete the more extreme races, but millions of fans around the globe follow them out of what I believe is a true desire to celebrate the potential of the human spirit.

The races themselves are probably the most difficult things most people will ever attempt. That's why they're so dramatic and why so many thousands of people watch; when months or years of training, hope, and pain are on the line, the tension is thicker than the Kona humidity. For most people in the Ironman, finishing in under seventeen hours will be their greatest achievement. Between the chaos of the swim, the agony of a bike ride with brutal hills and often blistering headwinds, the Hawaii heat, and the pure exhaustion of trying to run a marathon after you've already cycled 112 miles, some people cross the finish line on pure will alone. That's how powerful the pull of the Ironman is.

• • •

I had raced the Ironman in 2008, but I'd gotten in through the lottery system. In the eyes of some, I hadn't really earned my spot. In 2009 I qualified by finishing in third place as a Big Island resident at the Honu 70.3, a qualifying race. After doing the 2008 Ironman World Championship, Ultraman Hawaii in 2008, and Ultraman Canada in 2009, I was ready to show what I could do on the biggest stage in the triathlon world.

I have a story of my own that makes my journey to the Ironman unique. For starters, I have the use of my left arm only. My right arm has been paralyzed since I was knocked into orbit by a speeding car that ran a red light back in 1986, when I was just twelve years old. This means that in the 2.4-mile swim that starts the Ironman (and the 6.2-mile swim that begins the Ultraman), I swim with only one arm. It's hard enough to swim two miles with two arms, so you can imagine the effort it takes just to stay afloat with one, not to mention getting out of the water in less than two hours and twenty minutes.

But my arm is only one of the obstacles I've faced in getting to where I am today. I've often wondered if God allowed me to experience a life's worth of difficult times in order to build my character and make me more his servant. Having to depend on God has allowed me to grow closer to him and trust that he has bigger and better plans for me.

God led me to Hawaii and to the Ironman. Here the events of my past finally all came together and the picture became clear: my suffering, obsessive athletic training, and restless wandering toward the next thing around the corner were all leading me to this. I was meant to be an Ironman, an Ultraman—an everyman doing things that showed others how awesome God is and how they can blow past their own limitations if they listen to and trust him.

That's why I do it. That's why I push myself to compete with able-bodied athletes when I can use only one arm. I want them to see that I'm no different from them. I have some athletic gifts, but I'm not the greatest athlete in the world. My iron will is God's greatest gift to me. My true edge is that I refuse to stop. I refuse to give up. The wonderful thing is that you can do the same. We all can.

My revelation about my life has come in the last five years, since the Ironman became the center of my world. I'm finally able to see that during all those years I spent mad at God for taking everything away from me, he was actually giving me wisdom. He was teaching me how to be his instrument. Looking back, I can finally see a pattern of lessons he's been teaching me over the years.

Some of the most important and valuable lessons have come since I moved to Hawaii and started training for the Ironman in 2005. In that time I've faced greater struggles and tests of my will and commitment than ever before. The moments when we don't think we can surmount the obstacles, when we think we're going to break, when we feel the fear and *we keep going anyway*—those are God's teaching moments. Those are the moments when he imparts wisdom that can change our lives and set us on new paths of joy, meaning, and healing.

You may not aspire to do an Ironman, but odds are there is an endurance race of some kind in your life, whether it involves your health, family, career, or a dream that you're hesitant to chase. I hope the lessons I've learned will do for you what they've done for me: remind you that God is always with you, that you have more strength than you ever realized, and that if you don't stop, you *can't* be stopped.

1

YOU'RE ALREADY AT THE FINISH LINE

"The riders in a race do not stop when they reach the goal. There is a little finishing canter before coming to a standstill. There is time to hear the kind voices of friends and say to oneself, 'The work is done.'"
—**Oliver Wendell Holmes**

I had already swum more than five miles in the warm waters of Hawaii's Kailua Bay when I felt the first sting hit me. No big deal. A pinprick. *I can take that. Bring it on.* Then a few more. *Hmm. This might not be good.* I looked up at Bree Wee, my assistance kayaker (and a pro triathlete herself), who had been with me the whole way, and said as calmly as I could, "There's jellyfish around here—let's move out a bit!"

When you're on a long-distance swim, as in the first stage of the Ultraman, your kayaker is your guide and needs to know the currents on top of the water as well as under the water. Bree knows the waters of Kailua Bay as well as any-one; this is why I'd asked her to be my eyes for this race. I couldn't afford to waste precious energy on navigation; I just wanted to keep my head down and keep moving. Since I only have one arm to use in swimming, I have to use my legs to provide the extra horsepower, and that costs energy. I re-lied on Bree to keep me swimming in the right direction and to keep my energy level up with lots of verbal encourage-ment. She would yell things like, "You're doing great!" and "You look awesome!" from time to time. Bree is an angel.

The whole triathlon is like that. Even though you're rac-ing alone, you're never really alone. In the Ultraman race, a support team of at least two people accompanies each athlete over the entire course. In the Ultraman there are no aid sta-tions and very few fans because the course is way too big. The members of your support crew are your cheerleaders, your aid workers, and your eyes and ears. As the athlete, you are in control of telling them what you need, and they are there to provide for you, care for you, and push you. They are drill sergeants, psychologists, and nurses with one goal: to keep you pushing toward the finish line while preventing you from killing yourself. They supplement the work of a coach who has been overseeing your training regimen for the past year and helping you develop your race strategy and fine-tune your technique in swimming, running, and cy-cling. This is all necessary because you're racing against the best of the best on the international triathlon circuit.

More than fifty thousand athletes complete an Ironman triathlon somewhere in the world each year. About 1,800 com-pete in the Ironman World Championship alone. But only 36 triathletes compete each year in the Ultraman World Championship. These are some of the best-trained, most talented, and mentally toughest extreme athletes on the planet. I was honored simply to be competing in the same field with them.

But at that moment, I was more concerned with what I could feel—more and more jellyfish stings, like little electric shocks running up and down my body. The emergency boat had circled around to us and warned us that there was a school of jellyfish ahead. Several swimmers had been attacked already, and one swimmer had been pulled from the water. The officials on the boat told us to go farther out to sea in order to go around the jellies, but as I was swimming, I could look ahead and see hundreds of them moving toward me. With each stroke, I would swat the water to push a few jellyfish away so I could clear a path to swim. I was using my good arm to push them away and kicking harder with my legs so I could keep moving forward. The emergency boat was right behind me, almost as if the crew was waiting to haul me out. The stings became more frequent; despite my efforts, I was swimming right into the middle of the jellies.

Bree saw the trouble brewing. She shouted back, "I'm trying to get you out of here, but there are more and more." She was swatting the water with her paddle to clear a path for me, but a kayaker up ahead told her to stop; the motion was actually attracting more jellies. Bree started to sound worried, and that worried me. The rescue boat pulled alongside us. "Bring your swimmer to the right a little more," someone on board said. The race staff would try to help us and all the other support teams steer the athletes out of the cloud of poisonous jellies.

All of a sudden—*boom!* Thousands of stings were hitting me simultaneously—both legs, my good arm, my neck, all over. Frantically I tried to pull them off me. I screamed, "Bree, I'm getting bit!" I could feel tentacles on my legs and my neck, hundreds of them. I was starting to lose feeling in my left arm because of the venom. I felt like I was suffocating as the jellies hit me.

The rescue boat was behind me, and the officials aboard saw me starting to panic. Within seconds they were beside me. I screamed, "Get me in the boat, hurry, they are all over my neck!" They pulled me in, and I lay on a bench seat, quivering from the venom. Someone began to rub a salve all over me to neutralize it, which provided incredible relief. I could hear the driver of the boat on the radio saying, "Swimmer down! Swimmer down! We are on our way in! He's out of the race! We're bringing him in!" I could hear the boat start up, about to pull away toward shore.

Wait just a minute, I thought. *Bringing me in? This isn't the way this race is supposed to end, at mile five! What are you trying to teach me here, Lord? Please don't let this happen to me. I could see it if I was hurt or was not able to continue because I didn't train properly, but I have been training for this race the past twelve months. This was my time, I put in the work. Is this it?* All this went through my head in a few seconds, but it felt like hours. I knew that God had guided me to this point and seen me through the torture of training, and it was not supposed to end with me being carried back to land.

That was when I heard a voice in my head say, "Get up and get back into the water, and you're back in the race. Don't lie down here anymore." Bree must have seen my face because she shouted, "He's fine! Look at me, Jason! You're fine! You're going to be fine!" Her words brought me back to myself. I knew what I had to do. Before the rescue staff could stop me, I jumped off the side of the boat—right back into the same pool of jellyfish—and started swimming again. Let me tell you, I never kicked or pulled so hard in my life as I did for that last mile. My adrenaline was through the roof. I didn't know how fast or slow I was going; all I remember was kicking nonstop for the next hour. With every stroke I would look to my side and see Bree's face and her amazing smile. Every now and then she would throw her hands up in the air and yell, "You're doing amazing, Jason, woohoo!" and I would start to cry.

God had pulled me through another challenge. Soon Bree yelled, "There's the turn into the bay, Jason. We are almost there!" As I looked up I could see that we had passed my buddy Mike Rouse and his kayaker, and then I heard the voice of Steve King, the race announcer, say, "And here he is, folks, he just hit the turn buoy!" I headed for shore. I was back in the race.

• • •

It was November 27, 2008. I was in Kailua-Kona, competing against some of the best ultraendurance athletes from around the world—Brazil, Canada, Spain, the United States. It was the who's who of Ultraman. Previous Ultraman champions such as Andre Ribeiro, Peter Kotland, Erik Seedhouse, and Shanna Armstrong were there. I felt blessed and honored to be at the starting line with these amazing athletes who have done so much for the sport. The Ultraman World Championship is one of the most extreme triathlons on the planet. A race with a twenty-five-year history, it's a three-day event where to finish, you have to swim 6.2 miles, cycle 261.4 miles, and run a double marathon, 52.4 miles—more than double the length of an Ironman triathlon. To compete in one, you've got to be incredibly driven, inhumanly disciplined, or a little bit nuts.

Well, you do unless you're me. I do Ultraman because I feel called to this event. When God says, "Race," I say, "Where's the start?" On paper, the Ultraman seems crazy, but I don't look at the paper. I never count miles when I'm racing or training. I look at it like this. You have to start at point A and get to point B. You have a certain amount of time to get there or get a DNF—Did Not Finish. This has always been my way of thinking, all the way back to baseball during my freshman year of high school, when I showed up for the first day of practice able to use only one arm. Everyone was looking at me and wondering, "How is this kid going to catch the ball and then throw it?" I didn't worry about that. If a ball was hit to me, I got it to the base, simple as that. I started in left field my freshman year in baseball and was also the starting center on the football team at only 140 pounds. For me, sports have always been 20 percent physical and 80 percent mental. Twenty years later that hasn't changed.

Ultraman was the latest stage in a journey filled with tragedy, misfortune, and betrayal, but also with blessings beyond counting. I was competing because it was part of the destiny that God had revealed to me. I had gone into the race intending to be the first person with a physical challenge to finish. My drive came from knowing that I was fulfilling God's plan: to try and inspire other people who face their own challenges and aren't sure they can overcome them. I went to that starting line with the faith that God would have my back at every mile. Ultraman was my calling, and when you're called you either respond or hang up.

Just getting into the company of world-class triathletes, first at Ironman, then at Ultraman, had required some divine intervention. One day in early 2007 I was working out at the pool in Kona, training for my first Ironman race, the Arizona Ironman, to be held in April. A guy swimming next to me introduced himself as John. "I see you training every day," he said. "What you are doing is amazing." I was about to thank him for his kind words when he said, "Have you ever thought about doing the 2007 Hawaii Ironman through the lottery? Put your entry in. I have a feeling you will get in this year. I know the race director, and I'm going to put in a good word for you." Just like that. I've learned over the years that when that sort of good fortune drops in your lap, God is at work, so I always pay attention.

I submitted my entry to the 2007 Ironman World Championship lottery and hoped that it was in God's plan for me to be in that race. Thousands of people put their names in the lottery each year, and I knew it would be luck of the draw— or God's purpose. But I couldn't worry about that. I went on with my 2007 season. I raced the 2007 Arizona Ironman in Tempe—just twenty-five miles away from the place where, in 1986, I was hit by the car that changed my life forever. I wanted my first Ironman to be in Arizona as a way to say "I forgive you" to the young woman who hit me that night.

The day they released the results of the Ironman World

Championship lottery was the day of the Arizona Ironman race. As I prepped for the race I asked my best friend, Harold, to log on to the Ironman site during the day to see if I had won a slot. Talk about excited and nervous at the same time! That day in Arizona, I was focused not on the race I was in, but on the race I craved with every cell in my body. I ran the Arizona Ironman preoccupied with the Hawaii race. I crossed the finish line, and while my buddy was trying to congratulate me on finishing, all I could say was "Did I get in? Did I?"

His face fell, and my heart sank. "Dude, I couldn't find your name on the list. Sorry."

I felt devastated. I thought it had all been leading to this. But although my heart was set on the Ironman World Championship in October, I kept my sights on God's plan for that season. I went to New York and raced the New York City Triathlon, a regional race that would help me qualify for the world championship short-course race in Hamburg, Germany. I went on to race in Hamburg on Team USA, but the Ironman World Championship was still in the back of my mind. I tried to remember all I had gone through and all the times I had found God behind me. He was always opening a new door in preparation for the time when I found enough sense to quit complaining and walk through. *God is lining up something bigger than this,* I told myself. *It's just not my time yet.*

In October 2007, having failed to win a slot in the Ironman World Championship in Kona, I made plans to volunteer at an aid station for the run portion of the race. A few days before the race, my swim coach, Karlyn, was holding her annual prerace party. At the party I met several of Karlyn's friends who would be racing, including Kim Rouse.

Kim told me that her husband, Mike, was preparing to race the 2007 Ultraman World Championship, which is also held in Kailua-Kona. I lit up like a Christmas tree. I'd heard of the Ultraman before but didn't know much about it, so I asked Kim for details. Within thirty minutes she asked me to crew with her at Mike's race the following month. That's when I knew that God had something in store that was bigger and better than I could conceive of.

I joined Kim and Mike on Thanksgiving Day at the prerace banquet. I found myself sitting in a room with thirty-six athletes from around the world—former champions along with endurance athletes who had never raced an Ultraman before. Sitting there, I was overwhelmed with the desire to compete in this race.

Those three days crewing for Mike were some of the most memorable days of my racing career. When I wasn't helping Mike, giving him the support, fuel, and encouragement he needed, I was observing the course, becoming a student of Ultraman. But I was also learning what it really meant to be part of the Ultraman *ohana,* or family. The Ultraman is a tight, close-knit tribe, and when they want you to become part of the family, you're in.

On Day Three Kim, Mike, and I ran the final one hundred yards together. As we were crossing the finish line, the race director announced on the loudspeaker, "And running through with Mike Rouse is his wife, Kim, and his crew assistant, Jason Lester, who will be racing the 2008 Ultraman Event!"

My jaw dropped. I could barely believe what I was hearing. When I had signed up to crew, Kim had told the race director that I wanted to crew the race because I wanted to run the race in 2008. I hadn't filled out an application yet; it wasn't even available. But the race directors can choose anyone they want, and the race director, Jane Bockus, had just made the decision.

After shock and gratitude to God, my next reaction was that my previous plan for 2008 had to go out the window. This was an incredible new opportunity, and I needed a completely new strategy. All my focus and energy in the upcoming year would have to go toward the 2008 Ultraman. First I congratulated Mike and told him how honored I had been to crew for him for those three memorable days. After that I raced to catch a plane to Australia so I could compete in the Western Australia Ironman the following week. On the plane for the next nine or ten hours, I rethought my future. By the time I landed in Perth, I had the beginnings of my plan to become the first challenged athlete ever to complete the Ultraman. God's plan had finally become clear. Now it was up to me to make it happen.

● ● ●

I knew God was with me as I jumped back into that bay swarming with jellyfish. The race was already done; I just had to finish. No jellyfish stings were going to stop me. It would have been easier (and certainly less painful) to drop out and stay on the rescue boat and blame the jellies. Nobody would have thought less of me for quitting under those circumstances. But I couldn't. My adrenaline surged as soon as I hit the water. The stings also came back with a vengeance, but Bree slapped her kayak paddles to clear a relatively jellyfish-free path for me to swim to the finish line.

When does the human spirit give in to the limits of the human body and just close up shop? Or can we go as far as our spirit takes us? There was no way I could have prepared for what was happening, so I put it out of my head and just swam, using both legs to substitute for the propulsion that I couldn't get from my paralyzed right arm. I ignored the stings, pushed myself as hard as I could, and gradually escaped the jellyfish zone. Somehow, I kept getting stronger.

There's a big pink buoy that tells you when to make the left turn toward shore. I heard Bree scream, "There it is!" and I started hammering with both legs and my one good arm. I knew we were there. Here's the thing: I had been sprinting to shore for the last ninety minutes of the swim, not knowing how close I was to missing the cutoff time. You have only twelve hours per day to finish each leg of the race (Day One is a 6.2-mile swim and a 90-mile bike ride). At the end of the swim I was nearing the six-hour mark, the cutoff time for finishing the swim stage. As I turned around the buoy to head to shore, I looked to my left and could see that not only had I passed Mike Rouse, I'd done the swim in 5:22. I'd beaten the cutoff by thirty-eight minutes. This meant I had to bike the next ninety miles, uphill, within six hours and thirty minutes.

I don't think I've ever biked so hard before or since. I put my head down and forgot to drink and eat, but it was almost as if God was giving me natural energy to get to the town of Volcano by the cutoff time. At one point, about thirty miles before Volcano, it started raining hard. I was going about thirty miles per hour downhill through the rain—crazy, hazardous conditions. My crew was behind me, honking, telling me to slow down, but it was as if they weren't there. The sun started setting, and I started cooling off, and the next thing I knew I was catching up to cyclists. On one of my last stops, my crew said I had less than thirty minutes to make it to the finish line. I told them to go ahead. "I'll meet you in Volcano, and we *will* make the cutoff," I said. We made it with just fifteen minutes to spare.

• • •

One of the reasons that I made the cutoff despite the odds was that I kept my mind on the finish line. You *cannot* have negative thoughts in this sport. It's human nature to let them creep in once in a while, but if you do, you're done. Once you open the floodgates, you start running through all the things that can go wrong. *What if I get a flat tire? What if I fall? What if I cramp up in the water? What if I don't have what it takes?* From there, it's a short distance to giving up when the pain really starts. Because no matter how fit and well trained you are, there is always a point in every race where you begin to crash against your physical and mental limits. At that point, if you have any negative thoughts in your head, you're going to find an excuse to give up.

When I went to the starting line of Ultraman and looked into the ocean, I felt God telling me, "It's done." That was one of the things God had been trying to teach me my entire life. When I was a teenager, I would go for thirty-mile runs in the hills just for the heck of it. But in 2008 it became clear: one of the reasons I was able to endure such punishment and compete with a disability was because God had shown me that my *mind*—not my legs or lungs—was my greatest asset.

At the starting line I realized the race was *done*. I had already sacrificed and worked and steeled my will, and in my mind the race was run. I had finished. There was nothing to fear. I just had to drag my butt to where my spirit already was—the finish line. If I just focused on what I knew I had to do and took it one step at a time, I would get there. Just like that, there was suddenly no question that I would finish. It was one of the most amazing realizations I have ever experienced. That knowledge was the antidote for any negative thoughts creeping into my head. **You're already at the finish line.**

Every one of my races is already finished even before I reach the starting line because I have the will, knowledge, and discipline to do what I need to do to finish. The race is done in my mind. When that truth finally became clear to me, my jellyfish-interrupted swim and the rest of the 2008 Ultraman—along with every race since—became a matter of digging and kicking, pedaling, and putting one foot in front of the other. I knew that as long as I kept my mind at the finish, it would carry my body through jellyfish stings and Hawaiian heat, pulled muscles and gear snafus.

In my opinion a lot of Ironman competitors won't do Ultraman because there's a psychological barrier. They definitely have the physical endurance; they're already world-class athletes. But Ultraman is a totally different race. If you are going to do an Ultraman, your mind has to have the power to push past the pain. It's a completely different mental game. And it's not just triathlons—every sport is mostly about the mind. As baseball great Yogi Berra once said, "Ninety percent of this game is mental. The other half is physical."

Success in anything is about belief, but it's also about know-ing that you will reach your goal, whether it's finishing a tri-athlon or breaking one hundred in golf. When your mind is already at the goal, your body will not stop working and train-ing and pushing until it joins your mind in the winner's circle.

What is the difference between a professional athlete and an amateur? Sure, talent figures in; you either have it or you don't. But I'm sure you have watched incredible college athletes fail in the pro leagues while guys with fewer gifts and more mental discipline make it. That's the difference. We all have gifts; it's what we choose to do with our gifts that matters. In my sport my body is not my edge. There are triathletes with physical at-tributes that far exceed mine. But since childhood, I've always had a strong mind. I credit my dad, who was a standout football player in high school and college, with helping me develop my mind. My mind is my advantage. With it, I'm able to train my-self to be the best athlete I can possibly be.

God has given me a mind that lets me envision myself completing the swim, bike ride, and run. That's why even to-day I can go on a six-hour training ride or a thirty-mile train-ing run without any hesitation. I can "see" what the results of such rigorous and dedicated training will be. After all, I've already run the race in my head. The rest is just biomechanics.

• • •

The day after the Ultraman, there is an awards banquet. It's a wonderfully democratic event. In Ultraman, anyone who finishes is a champion, so each athlete gets to go up on stage and take five minutes to tell his or her story, including what happened during the race. Many people talk about why they entered Ultraman, and everyone has a moving story to tell. One guy, Warren, a close friend and training partner also from Kailua-Kona, fell and broke his back years earlier and was even electrocuted once. Another used to be a drug addict and used racing to help him recover.

When my time came to go up to the podium, I was so nervous I thought I might faint. I walked up there with my head down. I have never felt more humbled in my life to be in the company of people who knew what I had been through and who respected the fact that I had brought everything to my race. I have never felt more grateful to God that he chose me. When I could finally speak, holding back tears, thirty-four years flashed in front of my eyes. Being taken away from my mom by the state of Arizona when I was three, losing my father—I saw it all. The first words to come out of my mouth were, "Thank you. Thank you for embracing me as your own, thank you for coming into my life and treating me like family." For the first time since my father's death, I felt at home. I felt loved, like I had gained a new family, a family that I had never known.

There's a saying that goes, "God never gives you more than you can handle." I believe it. Think about all those characters in the Bible who did something amazing. They were humble people who had no delusions of grandeur. But when God chose them, they said, "Yes, Lord." God may only give us what we can handle, but the choice to handle it is ours.

God had a plan in mind for me from the day I was born, as he does for all of us. But though he chose me, it was my choice whether or not to listen to his call. It took a few years for me to finally pay attention. God knows the potential that lies within each of our minds; everyone has the power to say, "It's done," and just grab their goals. But each of us still has the freedom to use that power or reject it.

The knowledge that you're already at the finish line can change almost any aspect of your life. If you could visualize what you want as already achieved, how much could you accomplish? I'm sure that each of the brave Ultraman competitors I met at the awards dinner would understand the lesson. How else did they finish such a gut-wrenching race? Even more important, how did they endure such hardship just getting to the starting line? By saying, "It's done." That's exactly what keeps me going through today's toughest races, financial obstacles, and personal trials.

Imagine if you did the same with the challenges you face. You don't have to be an extreme athlete to visualize being at the finish line. This lesson applies to any situation in which the goal appears distant and the road ahead looks like too much for you to endure. Take getting in shape, for instance. Believe it or not, I used to shop in the husky section of the department store, so I know how hard it can be to lose weight and get fit. But when you can cast your mind ahead in time and be that slender, healthy person, transforming your body becomes a matter of finding out what to do and sticking to your routine. When you start seeing results, it becomes much easier to keep pushing. Triathletes train for a race in twelve to sixteen weeks; believe me, it doesn't take long to notice your endurance improving and your body fat dropping.

What about saving money and getting your finances in order? Experts say you're supposed to have at least six months' worth of expenses saved. But how are you supposed to do that? The same way that I run an Ultraman: one step at a time. What's so incredible about getting your mind to the finish line is that once you're there, all you have to do is make steady progress. It's not a race. You just need to save a little bit every month *and keep doing it.*

Starting a business works the same way; it's all about discipline and having a plan. Starting a company is more like a marathon than a sprint. Years ago I started my own art gallery in Los Angeles, so I know the routine: invest all your capital and time, try to anticipate the next steps, get blindsided, adapt, and keep going as best you can. It's a long uphill climb that can seem endless. But get your mind to the finish, and the steps needed to get there become clearer and less intimidating.

Unfortunately, I also know something about another common challenge, giving up drugs. I'm not proud of it, but once upon a time, before I let God into my life, I was abusing Ecstasy. But God showed me another way. He led me to the world of extreme racing, which I guess you could call a healthy, life-affirming addiction. The point is, whether you're hooked on drugs, food, or gambling, the road can look long, dark, and lonely. Moving your mind ahead in time to a point where addiction no longer controls you can give you the strength to take things one day at a time. You experience the joy and empowerment that will come when you're free.

Even the most incredible achievement is made up of small steps one after the other. The *Titanic* was assembled one rivet at a time. When you remember that, you become unstoppable. Just look at Dick and Rick Hoyt. Rick was born in 1962 with cerebral palsy, leaving him confined to a wheelchair. His father, Dick, did everything he could to make his son's life as normal and fulfilling as possible, and in 1977 he pushed Rick in his wheelchair as part of a 5K fundraiser. Dick, not a distance runner, finished next to last. But Rick was elated, and the father-son team soon started doing marathons: Rick rolling and Dick pushing.

Today, Team Hoyt has done marathons and even triathlons, with Dick towing his son in a boat as he swims! The two have written books and recorded DVDs, used their Hoyt Foundation to raise money to enhance the lives of the physically challenged, and they have even been inducted into the Triathlete Hall of Fame. Not bad for two nonrunners whom Boston Marathon officials didn't even want in the race.

The Hoyts' story is an incredible testimony to what you can do when you are open to God's path and just say, "It's done." When Dick pushed his son in that first 5K back in 1977, he didn't worry about not having the endurance to run a marathon; he wasn't trying to run a marathon. The day was about running three miles one step at a time. That goal was done in his mind; all he had to do was drag his body to meet his mind. They finished every race they entered in the same way. That's how ordinary people accomplish extraordinary things.

Racing is simple. It's life that's complicated. When I race, everything else in life fades into the background. The race is one big gift, a different world where I'm in control. Relationships, money, and business are the ultramarathon for me. That's why it's such an incredible blessing to have one thing to focus on: the finish line. When you realize that you are already at the finish, and you just go step by step, you can accomplish things no one ever thought you could.

Believe me, I know.

2

WHEN ONE STAGE ENDS, ANOTHER BEGINS

"Bad things do happen; how I respond to them defines
my character and the quality of my life. I can choose
to sit in perpetual sadness, immobilized by the gravity
of my loss, or I can choose to rise from the pain and
treasure the most precious gift I have—life itself."
—**Walter Anderson, American portraitist**

I don't remember flying one hundred and thirty feet through the air; I read that later in the police report. I don't remember landing on Bethany Home Road in suburban Phoenix with both of my legs broken. I don't remember the car that slammed into me or how my body demolished its windshield before being launched into the air. But one thing I know for sure: the path that led me to my life as an extreme athlete started on October 31, 1986. I was only twelve years old.

Years later I pieced the story together. On one corner of the intersection was a grocery store, and an eighteen-year-old girl who worked there was just getting off her shift as my friend Jerry and I pulled our bikes to the corner. Her friends had called to invite her to a Halloween party, and in her excitement and hurry she forgot to put on her glasses.

She pulled out of the parking lot about fifty yards away from the corner where I was waiting on my bike. Suddenly the light turned yellow, and, wanting to make the light, she hit the gas. She tore through the intersection just as I took off from the corner on my bike. In the center of the street our paths intersected. The car, going about forty miles an hour, slammed into me, knocking me out of my shoes and turning my beloved BMX bike into scrap metal. According to the police report, I flew up onto the hood and ricocheted off the windshield, flying a span approximately equal to the distance from home plate to second base in a major league park before slamming onto the pavement.

The next thing I remember is waking up in the middle of the road without any idea of what had happened. I was trying to get up. I was convinced that I was in the middle of traffic, sure that if I didn't get my butt off the pavement, I would get run over (never mind that I already *had* been). But as I tried to get to my feet, I kept falling back down. Jerry was screaming, "No, Jason, stay down! Stay down!"

People all around the intersection were shouting, "Call 911!" Cars were stopping, and I kept repeating, "No, I'm fine. No, I'm fine." But my left ankle and right knee were not cooperating with my brain. For good reason, as it turned out: they had both been shattered. I could hear sirens approaching, but before they arrived I blacked out.

The next thing I remember is the emergency room, a blur of nurses and doctors screaming, "Give me this!" and "Run this test!" just like in the television shows my buddies and I were so fond of watching. It would have been pretty cool except that I was the mangled patient they were working on. They must have given me some sedatives and painkillers because shortly after that everything went dark. I still didn't feel any pain, just confusion.

That was the beginning of a lonely, frightening time in intensive care. For about a week I drifted in and out of consciousness—more out than in. I was lying in a high-powered bed like a waterbed. I remember the bed like it was yesterday. I soon realized that it was a bed full of sand that kept me afloat because I had broken so many ribs I could not lie on my back or my side. I was doped up on industrial-strength painkillers and had no idea of the days or hours. Time had no meaning. But after a week, I started to understand what had happened to me. I didn't know the specific extent of my injuries, of course. I just knew that I couldn't move and my body didn't feel put together right. My left arm and both legs were in casts, and though I couldn't tell if my right arm was in a cast, I couldn't move it so I assumed that it was immobilized too. I didn't know what was broken and what wasn't. A tube was coming out of my right lung to drain the blood so that I wouldn't suffocate on it. I was a mess. Did I survive because I was young and athletic or because God was watching over me even though I didn't know who he was?

It was two weeks before they moved me to the pediatric floor. I was miserable. By this time I was in severe pain and would cry for hours until it was time for my next dose of medicine. I'll never forget the moment the doctor had to re-break my arm right in front of me because it was healing crooked. He told me to turn my head and that it would only take a second. Before the last word came out of his mouth— *snap!*—he had already broken it. Doctors walked in and out of my room—neurologists, psychiatrists, pulmonologists, and more. Finally I learned: a car had hit me. My doctor ran down the inventory: I had eighteen broken ribs, two broken legs, a broken left arm, and a collapsed lung. Worst of all, he told me that I had a paralyzed right arm. I was on morphine for the pain, so I didn't really connect with what he was saying. *Paralyzed? Sure, dude. Whatever.*

Later, when I was more alert, another doctor would break the terrible news: I would never be able to use my right arm again.

• • •

It was Halloween night. I had been at a Halloween party with twenty or thirty friends when my buddy Jerry Hahn and I decided we would ride our bikes to the Circle K convenience store and rent the movie *Rad,* a BMX-biking, boy-meets-girl movie we'd already seen about a hundred times. But we were pumped about it; it seemed like the perfect thing to do on a totally free, warm autumn night. So, still in costume, we got on our bikes and took off. Eventually we came to the intersection of 35th Avenue and Bethany Home. The Circle K was on the southwest corner; we waited on the northwest corner. The plan was simple: rent the movie, bike back to Jerry's house, throw it in the VCR, kick back on the couch, and drink soda and eat popcorn until we were ready to vomit.

We waited on the corner for the light to change, our bike tires touching. I was slightly in front, so I would be the first one to take off into the intersection. The difference between me or Jerry being in the middle of the street when disaster came calling was as small as the length of an adolescent's bike, about four feet. That still leaves me breathless when I think about it.

My life up to that point had been . . . complicated. Until I was three years old I had lived with my mother and my half brother, who was five years older. But my mom's problems with substance abuse kept getting worse. One day she abandoned my brother and me to go on a bender, locking us in the house. Well, we had a great time: we ate everything in the house, stayed up as late as we wanted, and felt free as birds. But when we started a fire inside the house to keep warm, the neighbors saw the smoke and called the police, who broke down the door. In short order my mother was in front of a family law court judge, and my brother and I were released into the custody of our respective fathers. I saw my mother only a handful of times after that until the day she died.

Life with my father was much, much better. Even though I was only three when my father gained full custody of me, I clearly remember the day. My brother and I had been placed in a foster home in Sedona until our fathers could win custody. The day my dad came to get me from that foster home, I felt an instant bond. It was as if I had met my teammate. During the next nine years I never left my dad's side. Everywhere he went, I had to go. I was like his shadow. I never really looked at him as a father; he was more like a brother. We were inseparable.

My father wanted to be nearby to help his mother, so we lived with my grandmother in the house where my father had been raised. My bedroom was the one my father had when he was my age, down the street from the same grade school and high school that he had attended. Charles Lester was a walking contradiction: a coach, struggler, Vietnam veteran, former college football player, former alcoholic, soul searcher, God knower, God seeker, an entrepreneur with an incredible heart. But all that mattered to me was that he loved me with everything he had. We were best friends. Although I had my own bedroom, we slept in the same bed until I was ten years old. He was the only adult in my life who ever made me feel safe—the only adult who never let me down. Dad became the center of my world.

Dad had been an aspiring football player with big dreams—until he was drafted at eighteen and sent to Vietnam. I don't know what happened to him over there; he would never talk to me about it. But I can't imagine it was much different from what a lot of vets of that war experienced: constant terror, watching buddies die all around you and wondering if you would be next, doing things that in peacetime would be unthinkable. I know that after he returned from 'Nam, he started drinking. After his death a buddy of his told me that my dad brought a lot of demons back from the war. When he did get home, he knew that any dreams he harbored of being a professional football player were over.

So his dreams became mine. To say that from the time I was six my life centered on sports is a ridiculous understatement. As soon as I was big enough to hold a baseball or wear a football helmet, my father's sole mission in life became turning me into a professional athlete, and I was only a bit less obsessed than he was. Every day he coached and I learned. I also grew to love running. My kindergarten teacher, Miss White, was a marathoner, and I would run with her when she trained in the mornings. But after a few years it became clear what path Dad had in mind for me: I was going to be a professional baseball player, probably a pitcher. By the time I was eleven or twelve, Dad was saying, "You know, you only have another few years before high school, and then after high school we'll keep working to give you the best chance of being drafted by a major league team."

I would look at him like he was joking. But he was serious. I felt a lot of pressure to outperform my peers. Dad went on to become Little League president, and I felt like I couldn't let him down. Even when I was young, I would go to bed at night with my bat in hand and my glove under my pillow. I would dream about playing in the big leagues. It's clear to me now that my father was living through me, but I didn't care. I wanted to make him proud.

Obviously, he was doing something right, because I was a six-time baseball all-star by the time I was twelve years old. But Dad wasn't an easygoing coach. He had a way of looking at me when I was out on the field that said, "If you screw up, your ass is grass. Don't ever embarrass me out there." He told me that if he ever saw me having fun on a baseball field he would pull me out of the game on the spot, and I knew he wasn't bluffing. He threw batting practice and I hit until I had blisters on my hands. He would hit ground balls to me until I couldn't bend over any longer and my shoulder ached from throwing, and then he would say, "No, you missed that one; we're going longer." For my father, playing sports was not fun and games. It was business. It was life. Heck, it was preparation for war.

He knew that the odds of any kid, no matter how talented, making it to the major leagues have always been impossibly long. So many obstacles can get in the way—injury, financial hardship, family troubles, or just losing the desire to work and sacrifice. If I didn't make it as a professional baseball player, Dad was going to make sure that it wasn't because of the things I could control: my discipline and preparation. So we worked and drilled and sweated, rain or shine, through blisters and pulled muscles.

I loved the training. I looked up to my father; he was my hero. In the six years that he was my coach and mentor, he taught me everything I needed to know for the rest of my life. *Be consistent. Never miss practice. No excuses. Never stop for anything.* Twelve years old is the time when a boy starts to become a man, and my dad passed on the lessons that made me a man.

That was why, when my body met the hard street on Halloween night, nothing could ever really be the same for us again. I think that was the beginning of the end for him, and that was when God showed me a lesson I didn't understand until many years later.

• • •

I spent three months in the hospital. When word got out that I'd been T-boned by a car, friends from school started dropping in to see me. My middle school teacher would come over and ice my head and help me deal with my headaches. My Pop Warner football team was preparing for the regional championship football game, so my teammates dedicated that game to me and gave me the game ball after we won the state championship later that year. Still, as the weeks passed, I started to feel like I was in a black hole. Everything hurt. My head was constantly pounding. My doctors had started cycling my medication: instead of giving me painkillers around the clock, they would give them to me only when I complained. I would sit and cry for hours because everything hurt so bad. In order for me to start rehabilitation and get my strength back, they had to wean me off the meds. It was grueling. Rehabilitation, once it began, was its own kind of torture.

But I don't think I was the one who took the worst beating during that difficult time. It was my father. My broken bones would heal, even if my right arm would not. But my dad's dreams for me seemed to be over. As I lay in the hospital bed, I could see him pacing the halls. Often he would leave the room and return with tears in his eyes. At the time I didn't know why, but I now look back and realize that my dad was heartbroken. He had spent virtually every waking moment of the last six years dedicated to the proposition that I would play professional baseball. I was (or had been) right-handed. That arm was now dead weight. It was clear that his dream was over.

Dad stayed with me in the hospital. He had a cot next to my bed and slept there every night. But he spent a lot of time out of my room, and though he told my grandmother that he was going to work, he didn't. He headed down to the hospital lobby to sit on the stairs, staring into space. He fell into a depression. When I got out of the hospital, our relationship had changed. When I was in rehabilitation, the athlete-to-athlete bond we had shared was gone. He had become my caretaker. He was feeling sorry for me, but I knew that he was feeling just as sorry for himself.

About seven months after I left the hospital, one hot summer night, my father died of a heart attack at age thirty-nine. Early that evening he had a minor heart attack at the house but didn't go to the hospital. Three hours later he had a major heart attack and finally went to the emergency room. The doctors stabilized him and checked him into a cardiac care room for observation, but later that night he had a third heart attack and passed away.

When I got the news, I went numb. My father, dead? I had just started to get my life back after my accident, and now I had lost the one person who was everything to me? It was impossible to comprehend. It was so unreal that for years I couldn't cry or grieve. In a matter of months my entire life had been destroyed. My grandmother became my legal guardian. I didn't know God back then, and after my father's death I had no idea if he existed at all. If he did, I couldn't believe he would take away a young boy's ability to use part of his body and then follow that up by taking his father.

But in looking back over the years since his passing, I've

found the unmistakable signs of God's will working in my life even then: **When one stage ends, another begins**.

Relationships, jobs, opportunities—they flow into our lives, and they flow out too, sometimes predictably, sometimes tragically. When they leave, we're programmed to think of the transition as a loss, something painful to be mourned. That's what I did at first when my father died and my arm was paralyzed. But what if those losses and good-byes are something else? When a person passes from our lives through death, divorce, a breakup, or just moving away, it's not simply a tragedy. Just like an Ironman triathlon happens in stages, life comes in stages, and the departure of a person or an occupation is the beginning of a new stage. It's God clearing space in our lives for something to enter that serves his purpose. When someone loses a job because of a recession, it can be frightening. But what if God is simply making room in that person's life for a new and greater opportunity to serve him and know real joy? That's what I realize now that God was doing in my life back in 1986.

My accident changed everything for me and for my dad. My so-called destiny as a baseball player was history, but would I have served the Lord as a pro ballplayer? I don't know. If I'd made it to the major leagues, it's more likely that I would have collected a fat paycheck, enjoyed the life of a big league ballplayer, and told myself I was content. That would have been the end of it. I would never have gotten to know God, never have placed my life in his hands.

Instead, painful and difficult as they were for a twelve-year-old, my losses were God's way of preparing me for something else. My father drove me to become a better athlete than I ever could have been on my own. He instilled a fighting spirit and fierce discipline in me, things that have served me well as an extreme athlete. But another stage of my journey was due to begin, and new guides were needed in my life.

Who were the people who entered my life at this new stage? My neighborhood buddies. I'd started making friends in junior high school, and by this time I had five of them who were like brothers to me: Mike Brown, Fred Hunt, Steve Claiborne, Joe Biondo, and Jason Woodburn. When my casts came off, they were there for me. They made sure that I still felt like a part of my baseball and football teams, went to all the games, and stayed in the loop. They didn't baby me. They'd say, "Let's go, gimp. Come on." That was exactly what I needed. Somehow they knew it.

We all lived within a mile of each other, we all had BMX bikes, and we all played football, basketball, and baseball. We did everything together—*everything*. After Dad died I was lost for a while. But because of these guys I was still part of the crew. In the morning before class we'd play football, after school we'd play basketball, then baseball. I would play with one arm, and they wouldn't give me any breaks or go easy on me. They treated me like one of the guys, which was what I so desperately wanted to be again.

Mike was the standout athlete of the group. At twelve, he was a legitimate badass, dominating any sport that he set his sights on—wrestling, football, baseball, and basketball. I remember when he picked up BMX racing and made the other kids look like they had never raced before. After my accident I went everywhere with Mike. He even wore my Pop Warner jersey under his own jersey at football games. We became like brothers. When it was time for me to get back out on the baseball field a year after the accident, Mike looked me in the eyes and told me that he would have my back through it all. The year I returned, at thirteen, I not only started in left field but also made the all-star team.

Without my friends keeping me going, none of that would have happened. They tied my shoes for me and did whatever I needed so that I would be able to play. Every day before football practice, Fred Hunt would put my pads on for me in the same locker room where my father had once laced up his pads. I felt honored to be a part of the Alhambra High School legacy.

These guys had my back. It is still the most amazing act of pure love I have ever experienced. I wouldn't have had the confidence to play if I had been left on my own. I wasn't sure enough of my ability to compete with one arm, and I was lost without my dad to teach me. But my five BMX brothers didn't let me quit. These five guys knew that I was one of them; they were not going to let me sink into the darkness.

They ushered in a new stage where I discovered that I could still be an athlete. I didn't have to be confined to the sidelines because of my arm. This is why God is so amazing: it wouldn't serve his purpose for me to sit in my room feeling sorry for myself or believing that the only worthwhile way to be an athlete was to go to the major leagues, the NFL, or the NBA. God brought these influences into my life so that I wouldn't give up.

There's no question in my mind that this new stage set

me on the course to the Ultraman. It showed me that I still had the desire to compete, could still push myself to outwork everyone else, and had the dedication and determination to never stop. It showed me that what makes an athlete isn't a throwing arm or jumping ability, but will, heart, and desire.

I went on to play baseball and football, and in my freshman year my baseball coach asked me if I'd ever considered track or cross-country. I laughed and responded, "I hate running. That's why I run so hard and so fast during practice, to get it over with." But something inside me wanted to try it. The summer of my freshman year, I joined the cross-country team and showed up at practice wearing shoes that must have weighed fifteen pounds while the other guys were sporting feather-light cleats. My learning curve was steep.

In my sophomore and junior years I focused more on running. Was this the start of my running career? Was I running from something or running toward a greater purpose? Back then I had no idea. Now, I honestly feel it was God revealing my life's calling to me. After my junior year I started getting interested in biathlons, which combine cycling and running. In the next four years I would compete in over forty biathlons. By the time I was eighteen, I was ranked number two in the state of Arizona.

● ● ●

Since those adolescent years, many more people and opportunities have passed into and out of my life. Many of the departures were painful. Mike Brown, my best friend and superathlete pal, committed suicide three years after my father's death by driving a car off a bridge after a girl broke

Visiting Grandma Frank and Grandpa Billie Jean in Phoenix. Even though I never had a relationship with my mother, her parents always played a role in my life.

With my
dog Lady on
Christmas Day.

Baseball was my life growing up. Here I am with my all-star team celebrating a win.

In 1986, my Pop Warner football team won the state championships. I was heavier than kids my age, so I had to play with the older kids. When my dad died, I got scared that I might die of heart disease, too. Today I weigh as much as I did then.

Good friends Jason and Jenny Brantel visiting me in the hospital. Every other limb had a cast on it but I still didn't believe my right arm was paralyzed.

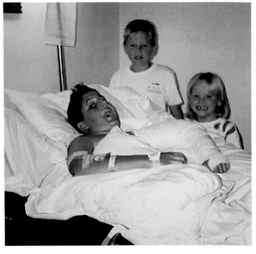

Battling the Queen K Highway at the 2009 Ultraman World Championship.

With my little buddy Christian, who ran down Ali'i Drive with
me at the 2009 Ironman World Championship.

Swimming 6.2 miles at the 2009 Ultraman World Championship.

At the 2009 Ultraman World Championship finish line with my soul brother Rich Roll.

Onstage at the 2009 Ironman World Championship receiving a recognition award given to the challenged athletes who finished the race.

Crossing the finish line at
Ultraman Canada.

Coaching my friend Steve in the swim in preparation for his first
Ironman. Once homeless and an alcoholic, he worked with me to
turn his life around. He hasn't raced in a triathlon, but today his
life is back on track.

Kailua-Kona, Hawaii, my home and my sanctuary—the perfect environment for training and the place where I feel most at peace.

The moment that drives me to swim 6.2 miles, bike 261.4 miles, and run 52.4 miles—the finish line at the Ultraman World Championship.

The man behind the plan—my coach, Dave Ciaverella—and me at the 2009 ESPYs. When I accepted the award, I thought about Dave and all the other people who had helped me train, supported me during races, and refused to doubt me. I thought about all the people who voted for me and about the people in Kona who had adopted me as a son and cheered me on. I accepted the award for all of them.

I was a guest of honor at an Arizona Diamondbacks game following my ESPY win. At the ESPYs, I was surrounded by superstars. Brian Clay, the 2008 decathlon Olympic gold medalist, sat in front of me. To my side were members of the U.S. Olympic soccer team. I could see Michael Phelps, Kobe Bryant, LeBron James, and Tim Tebow. Samuel L. Jackson was at the podium as master of ceremonies. My head was spinning from the entire experience. When they announced my win, I just praised God and thanked him.

his heart. Years later I watched my daughter, Katana, carried crying from my home in Kona as my marriage unraveled. Some stages of my life ended harshly and abruptly, leaving me wondering how the story could ever make sense.

But with the new eyes that God has given me, I can see what I couldn't see before: that every loss is followed by a new blessing. The only condition is that I leave it in God's hands and trust him to bring me something new that moves me farther down his path toward greater glory, peace, and prosperity.

We all experience losses. It's part of being human. You may have been laid off from a job that you held for twenty years. You may have watched a relationship fall apart or seen disease take the life of someone you loved. Life can be like an international airport: a never-ending cycle of departures and arrivals. As I've known for years, we have little control over the things that happen to us. But we do have control over how we *respond* to what happens. That's the key to turning this lesson into a source of strength and joy.

The fact that life comes in stages is like a spiritual law working to maintain the balance in our lives. Like all laws, it's immutable; the stages of life happen whether we want them to or not. So when your company lays you off, it is inevitable that God will bring some new opportunity to you to take the place of what's gone. The big question is will you see that new opportunity and respond to it in a positive way? That's the key for all of us. When things go against us, we have to learn to get past our grief, anger, and self-pity and realize, "Wait a second, something new is about to come and fill this void in my life. I'd better be on the lookout for it."

Such an attitude doesn't come naturally. Believe me, once my father died, if my five buddies hadn't come along to pull me out of my shock and drag me back into sports—back into life—I don't know where I might have ended up. I doubt I would be competing against the best extreme athletes in the world. I needed my buddies' help to accept the next stage of my race. God doesn't force things upon us; he merely shows us the door. It's our choice whether or not to walk through.

If you could change how you view the losses in your life, wouldn't that change everything? Let's say you're laid off from your job. Your instinct is to panic because you now have a mortgage and credit card debt and no money coming in. You might want to lash out in anger at your employer, the government, or whoever else gets in your way, or just feel sorry for yourself.

But what if you could react differently? What if you took God's lesson to heart, and instead of freaking out when your job came to an end, you saw it as a sign that one stage was ending and another was about to begin? What if you ended up getting a better job, finding an opportunity to start your own business, or building a new career doing something that brought you real fulfillment?

Let's say you endure the painful breakup of a long-term relationship. For many people, this is a reason to sink into a funk of dark depression. They mope. They lose weight—or gain it. They become hermits. Do these things help? Of course not. But if you could perceive the breakup not as a termination but as a transition, you would be on the lookout for the blessing coming your way. Perhaps it would be a chance to grow and become a better person before your next relationship. Or maybe it would be the chance to meet your soul mate, someone you might otherwise have overlooked. When we change how we see the events of our lives, we change the outcome.

Knowing that a void is just a space for God to fill can change how we respond to the ups and downs of life. It gives us peace of mind. It fills us with hope.

• • •

Eighteen years after my accident, I did something I needed to do: I forgave the young woman who hit me with her car. I couldn't have done it before gaining this new understanding about the different stages of life. But when I looked at how events have played out—my accident, my father's death, my friends pulling me back into life all leading to the inspiration that so many have drawn from my paralyzed right arm—I started to wonder if the driver wasn't simply the first person to be guided by God into my life. I certainly wouldn't have asked for things to be set in motion the way they were, but the fact remains that the next and defining stage of my life began that night because of her.

That was why at age thirty I sent a letter of forgiveness to her. I knew from reading the police report that the girl, panicked and freaking out, sped off with my hair embedded in her windshield. She knew she had been speeding, was not wearing her glasses, and had run a red light. She knew that she was in *big* trouble. Fortunately, some witnesses chased her down and told her that she had to go back to the scene because she'd just annihilated some poor kid.

So I sent her a letter. The message was simple: "I forgive you." One of the things people told me I had to do after my dad died was to forgive him for leaving me. This young woman hurt me in a way that was much worse than my father leaving me, but I also knew that she had played a role in my being transformed into the person I had become. I needed to acknowledge that.

God said that you have to forgive the people who have wronged you. I could not have forgiven her before I came to God, but afterward it was surprisingly easy. The letter I wrote was graceful and peaceful, with no anger whatsoever. In it, I told her that I needed to do this to move on to the next stage in my life. I never heard back from her, and I have no idea if she ever got the letter. But that doesn't matter. I wrote it for myself.

3

BUILD YOUR LABORATORY

"He who ignores discipline despises himself, but whoever heeds correction gains understanding."
—**Proverbs 15:32**

I will never forget the day I saw my first Ironman World Championship: October 16, 2004. I had arrived in Hawaii only the day before, as luck would have it. One of the angels of my life, Renee, had brought me to the islands, though not for the Ironman. Renee and I had met in 2002 in Los Angeles, fallen in love, and by February 2004 had a gorgeous little girl, Katana. Renee is from Hawaii, and just three months after Katana was born, her parents came to visit us in Los Angeles. At the time, I was working intense hours at my job at a sports marketing agency and spending the rest of my waking hours managing exhibitions at the Manhattan Beach art gallery I'd opened as a way to decompress from my job. I was not around very often.

Renee told me that she felt alone and homesick, so I guess it shouldn't have been a surprise when I came home one day in April 2004 and found her and Katana gone. Renee's parents had invited her to move back to Hawaii to live with them, and she'd accepted. She told me that when I was no longer controlled by work, I could come out and visit.

I didn't know anything about Hawaii. I actually thought it was one island, if you can believe that. But I knew I wanted Renee and Katana, so in October 2004 I took a fateful flight to the Big Island, met Renee's family, and had the experience that would change my life.

It had been my dream for years to see the Ironman World Championship in Kona, on the Big Island, in person. Of course I knew about the Ironman. As I've said, I had been the number two–ranked biathlon racer in Arizona when I was eighteen, and the love of running and long-distance competition was wired into my genes. In recent years, in an effort to get some balance in my life and keep myself healthy despite my stressful work, I had started running marathons again, and I harbored a vague desire to actually compete in a triathlon. But I was a slave to my work and couldn't find the time to train. Even so, I was slowly becoming absorbed by the world of extreme distance athletes, and I couldn't wait to watch the Ironman up close and personal. It didn't occur to me that God might have brought me to Hawaii for exactly that purpose.

That day I drove west from Hilo to Kona, and my excitement could have lit up half the island. Parking on the day of the race was a disaster, so I left my car a long distance away and walked down to the spectator area. As I strolled up the main drive among the early morning crowds to the transition zone where the athletes would begin the swim stage, I started to cry. I didn't know why. The emotion that hit me was overwhelming. But it was more than that. As I got within sight of the starting line, an almost suffocating longing washed over me. I could barely stop myself from falling to my knees and sobbing right on the spot.

I found a vantage point from which to watch the start and felt something boiling inside me. *Jason, this is you, Jason, this is you.* In the past few years I had been wondering what my purpose was and not finding any answers. Was I meant to be a gallery owner or a sports agent? What did God want from me? I had no clue. But as I watched the start of the Ironman, everything came together. It was like I'd been standing too close to a painting and seeing only brushstrokes and blobs of color, then I stepped back and suddenly took in the whole picture in vivid color. I saw all the roads God had directed me down: my athletic training, my father's death, which scared me into training even harder as a distance athlete, my relationship with Renee, which brought me to Hawaii, a place I never would have come to otherwise, and more. It all made sense; it culminated right here.

For the next nine hours I cried like a baby as I watched these incredible athletes punish their bodies over a 2.4-mile swim, 112 miles on the bike, and a full marathon, 26.2 miles. I saw the discipline. I saw the passion. I saw the courage to gut through the agony. But more than anything, I was touched by all the brothers, sisters, husbands, wives, and kids supporting their Ironman athletes on this day. It was the kind of family that I had dreamed about. I saw the love and adulation that enveloped each athlete who reached the end of the run stage, when the announcer would say, "You are an *Ironman!*" I craved that with all my soul.

All I could think about was getting in there with them—feeling the pain, the fatigue, and the thrill of joy at reaching the finish. When the race was over, I said to myself, *I need to do this. I need to structure my life so that I can train for this event.* I called my old childhood buddy Jeff Fontenot and said to him, "What do you think about me doing the Ironman?" He said, "Jason, you *are* the Ironman. What's stopping you?"

That's all it took—one person believing in me—for me to do this. I knew I needed to quit my job, close my art gallery, sell my belongings, and do whatever it took to get back to Kona and become an Ironman. It wasn't a choice; it was the purpose of my life, newly revealed to me.

● ● ●

But getting myself to Hawaii full-time was easier said than done. When I realized how much I wanted to attempt the Ironman, I faced some decisions. I still had friends and my gallery in Los Angeles, but I also wanted to be closer to Renee and Katana. Finally in October 2005 I relocated to the Big Island, and Renee and I married. This was the chance to build the family I had never known as a child.

Still there were many loose ends to tie up in California: my job, my gallery, and so on. So we flew back to Los Angeles as a family for a "temporary" stay that ended up lasting all of 2006. Finally, in December of that year, I was ready to cut my ties and go back to the islands. We kept the gallery because I had a lease and we needed the income. But everything else we left behind. I was, as they say on the World Poker Tour, "all in."

Renee and I got a small condo in Kona in late 2006. Shortly after that, I hired Masters Swimming world champion Karlyn Pipes-Neilsen as my swimming coach and began training to fulfill my dream.

I had decided that my first Ironman would be in Arizona in 2007. But the time and focus that it takes to train for an Ironman—twenty to twenty-five hours a week—started to wear on my relationship with Renee. I was so focused and determined to finish the race that I was putting her and my daughter second. There wasn't much room for anything else in my life. When Renee saw how much I was training, she decided that she would stay with her parents in Hilo.

By February 2007 it had become too much. Renee and I separated. I'll never forget the day I came home from training and she had all of her things packed. With Katana in her arms, she said, "God has a huge calling on your life, and I need to step out of it." She eventually made the decision that she and I should not be together.

I was in pain and confused about my family even as I was exhilarated about progressing with my training. I knew that God had called me to become an Ironman, but didn't God also want me to have a strong family? Was he going to take more people that I loved away from me?

From that point on I lived in the center of the strangest contradiction. On one hand, I was kicking butt in my Ironman training. I was developing into a triathlete and getting in the best shape of my life. Doors were flying open left and right: I was getting sponsors, I had an amazing set of coaches, and a film production company soon approached me to do a motion picture about my journey. I felt like I was finally on the road that God had been pointing me toward all those years. On the other hand, all I wanted was my relationship with my wife and child. The divorce dragged on for a year of tension and pain. The only way I could deal with it was to train harder and harder.

It hurts that I'm not there every day with my daughter and that Renee and I couldn't make things work. But Renee played such an important part in my life. Most obviously, she brought me our daughter, Katana, but she also brought me to Kona and the Ironman. If I hadn't known Renee, I might never have seen the race and never have known my true calling. Yet it was more than that. She brought me to a place where I feel like I belong. The culture of Ironman is so strong that to be single-minded about it is normal. The Ironman athletes and supporters understand my near-obsession with extreme training and pushing myself beyond all sane limits. Without Renee, none of this would have happened.

Today, Renee and I live on opposite sides of the island, and I see my sweet Katana as often as I can. But I have no doubt that Renee was an angel who came into my life to bring me a blessing—to take me to another stage. I've told her in the past that despite all we've been through, she's still my angel. I say it to her again here. She is my biggest prayer warrior; she continues to pray that God's will be done in me.

• • •

Moving to Hawaii was also the start of my Laboratory.

When friends say they haven't heard from me for a while, I can say I'm "in the lab" and they always know what I mean. The Laboratory is my custom-created training environment—a lifestyle, really. To do what I do, I have to be single-minded, putting my complete focus, twenty-four hours a day, on the things that get me ready mentally and physically for a punishing race. The Laboratory is everything around me—my living space, the town I live in, my training regimen, my diet, my coaching, my friends, my time with God—all calibrated to achieve the goal of getting me successfully to the finish line of an Ironman, Ultraman, or other extreme race.

Anyone can create their own Laboratory. Unfortunately, too many people overlook this important step on their journey to achieving their dreams. It might be because they aren't ready to be "all in," and they think that focusing so intensely on what they want will force them to sacrifice in other areas of life (as I did). Or maybe they don't believe they have the right to take such a drastic step. But I believe each of us, each of you, has the right to create an environment that allows you to become the person God wants you to be. That means choosing who you do and don't associate with, how you spend your time, and how you arrange your daily routine. In my experience, by doing this, you give yourself the best chance of success.

The Laboratory is whatever you need to realize the potential that God has placed in you. My lab is pretty extreme, but that doesn't mean yours has to be. If you're a would-be writer trying to turn out that great novel rattling around in your head, maybe your Laboratory consists of a detached office where you can be completely alone to write for two or three hours after the kids go to bed. If you're trying to lose weight, your lab might consist of a house purged of unhealthy food, a tribe of positive people all chasing the same goal who hold you accountable, and a personal trainer who kicks your butt. Every person's Laboratory will be different, but all are guided by the same principle: it's the environment where your needs come first. Call it a little enlightened self-interest in the service of God.

The lab is my sanctuary because I feel most at peace when I'm training. At the heart of my Laboratory are the people who support me and whose attitude makes the path easier. I'm a firm believer that to be the best you can be (whether you're an athlete or not), you need to be around people who believe in you. Back in 2006 I knew what it was going to take for me to achieve these outrageous goals, and I still know that for me to be the best Christian, father, athlete, friend, and nephew, it takes an environment built around the right people. I can't associate with people who go to bars and drink. I can't associate with people who do drugs. I can't associate with unhealthy lifestyles because I'm trying to be the best I can be. I know what unhealthy lifestyles do to people; I come from a background where one parent was an alcoholic and another was a drug user.

Positive vibes? I thrive on 'em. My lab, whether it's my training environment or social environment, has to be filled with positive, life-affirming people for me to function to the best of my ability. That's another reason I've chosen to live in Hawaii, besides that fact that my little girl lives here. Living in Kona near the Ironman course (the finish line is literally a few blocks from my home) allows me to focus on something other than climbing the corporate ladder and making money, which is what life in Los Angeles was like. Living here allows me to be closer to God and my purpose. Since moving here, I've watched my life change. I walk around town and know everyone, and everyone knows me. Kona has become my home. My friends there, mainly other Ironman and Ultraman athletes, are my family.

When you build your Laboratory, choosing who and what to exclude are just as important as choosing what to include. I've had to cut certain friends out of my life and end relationships because they only brought negative emotions into my world and harmed my efforts. You can love your neighbor and still not want to associate with your neighbor—at least, not during a stage of life when there's a lot at stake. Going into the lab means policing your associations and being ruthless about removing—subtly or overtly—anyone who might prevent you from reaching your goals.

When you build your Laboratory, you'll have to make the same decisions about what to sacrifice. In my experience, intensely pursuing any goal means having to make at least some sacrifices. But sacrifice isn't always a bad thing. Sometimes the things you sacrifice are actually things that do you harm, such as giving up burgers and fries if you're trying to get into shape.

A Laboratory can be a physical location set apart from every other place in your life, like a gym, an office, or a music studio. It can be a span of time devoted exclusively to working on yourself and making progress toward the finish line. It can be both. Whatever constitutes your lab, the one requirement is that when you're there, you need to be dedicated completely to your own mental and physical preparation. When I train, I'm 100 percent in the lab. There's no halfway.

Is there a personal cost to building a Laboratory? I'd be lying if I said there wasn't, but I believe that it's a cost worth paying. In peeling away the unnecessary layers of life to get down to the essentials of who God wants you to become, you're also going to scrub away some toxic relationships. When you commit more of your time, energy, and focus to the single-minded pursuit of something that contains the meaning of your life, not everyone will understand. The people in your circle who are generous of spirit will bless you, not feel insulted. These are true friends and supporters who only want the best for you, even if it reduces their place in your life for a while.

Your retreat into the lab could drive some people from your life—maybe temporarily, maybe forever. I think you've got to be strong when that happens and know that God is moving you into a place of richer, more complete relationships so you can better serve his purpose. If your passionate chase of something that brings you joy forces some people from your life, then they probably did not belong there in the first place.

• • •

Part of my Laboratory is proper nutrition. I've been a vegetarian for twenty years, and in 2009 I became a vegan, eating
only a plant-based diet. I eat from the same selection of
healthy foods every day. I wake up and have a Vega brand
smoothie with fruit. I have my first training session, which
might be a four-hour bike ride or ten-mile run, then I go to
the juice bar for eight ounces of wheatgrass and an acai
berry smoothie. Lunch is always tons of veggies and greens,
and I love almond butter with gluten-free breads. I drink
plant-based smoothies that have hemp and flaxseed oil in
them. I eat a couple of avocado sandwiches on hemp bread
each day to get my healthy monounsaturated and polyun-
saturated fats, and then it's another training session, either in
the pool or at the gym. For dinner it's always a huge green
salad and brown rice with tofu.

The only time I vary that routine is during the few weeks
a year I give myself to relax and slack off, usually right after
a major race when I know I don't have any big races coming
up for a while. Then I go a bit easier on myself, but I still
avoid all junk and processed foods. I still think like the
pudgy adolescent who had to watch every calorie rather than
the rail-thin triathlete, which is probably why I stay skinny.
But I think it's important to go easy on the discipline once in
a while just to give my mind a break. Every now and then,
you need to reward yourself for all the hard work. Believe
me, there's nothing sweeter than a big bag of organic corn
chips, which I can kill with a bowl of guacamole.

But when I'm in the lab, I try to eat as organically as possible. Ninety percent of my diet comes from whatever is

grown from God and from the earth. That's why I eat lots of fresh almonds and fresh fruits and vegetables. I don't eat anything processed or fried, and of course I don't eat meat. Once a week, if I have a craving for something outside my diet, I'll indulge myself as a reward. But the leaner and cleaner I eat, the better I perform, the more mental clarity I have, and the simpler my life is. So even though my diet might seem boring, the results it produces are anything but boring. My mind and body feel like a million bucks. Makes me wonder how much happier we would be as a society if we just quit eating garbage and went back to eating the foods that God intended our bodies to run on: fresh fruits, vegetables, nuts, herbs, and roots.

I created my Laboratory in Kona only four years ago, but I started laying the foundation for it when I was twelve years old and my dad died. At thirteen, I weighed 140 pounds. I was heavy for my height, and I was worried that I would suffer from heart disease and die young like my father. That's when I made the decision to clean up my diet and live a healthier life. God works in and through us, and change is a process, not a flash of lightning. It's taken twenty-three more years to bring me to where I am today and make me the person I am now.

God molds us, and it's slow work. Believe me, relentless discipline is not easy. I have to work on staying in the lab every day, no matter how tempting it becomes to blow off a workout or just stop altogether. But when you find your purpose, the discipline becomes easier. You already know what works for you. You already know what's right for you. God put that knowledge in you. Are you listening?

• • •

We all have goals. We all have paths in life that call to us. We may have settled into a comfortable place where we can jam the earbuds in our ears, turn up the music, and pretend we don't hear our calling. But it doesn't go away. Too often people decide that they can't have their dreams because pursuing them would take too much time, disrupt their family life, force them to quit their jobs, or alienate friends who don't understand what they're doing. But when you feel a passion for something that keeps you awake at night and fills you with longing, that is God's voice speaking to you. You owe it to yourself to pay attention and try to follow the path that he has cleared for you. Rather than abandon any aspirations to make your divine vision a reality, try to **build your own Laboratory.** Take the first small steps toward creating an environment around yourself that will empower you to follow your dream. If your efforts lead to only modest progress, that's much, much better than nothing.

Your path probably won't look like mine. Let me say this loud and clear: you don't need to leave your previous life behind to start living a new one. You might decide you *want* to change everything, like I did. You could quit your job, move to a strange place, sever all your old relationships, and live off pennies and dryer lint in order to write your novel or just meditate and discover the secrets of the universe. But that's pretty extreme. That was God's path for me, but your path and your experience are going to be different. Remember that the goal isn't to throw out everything and everyone from your current environment just for the sake of doing it.

It's to create the space, time, motivation, and support you need so that when God opens a door, you feel free to walk through.

Here's the key to building your lab: whatever you do, arrange it so that you have no choice but to make progress toward your dream. Create a structure that makes it almost impossible for you *not* to write a chapter of your novel or complete your workout. A Laboratory doesn't work without accountability. I break my day into a strict schedule that's impossible not to follow. I cut other activities—hikes, dinner and a movie with friends, extra travel—almost entirely out of my life so that the only thing that can fill the void of time is training, training, and more training. I even sold my car when I moved to Hawaii so that I would be forced to ride my bike to the pool, the gym, and the grocery store. That's ten extra training miles a day (and it lets me live cheaper)!

You've got to do the same thing if your own lab is going to pay dividends. You might not need to relocate and become a hermit. You might instead keep your job and maintain your circle of friends but instead carve out two hours each day that are completely yours to work out, compose music, or do whatever furthers your passion. There are only two rules.

The first rule is that the time is yours and is completely dedicated to whatever pursuit God has laid out before you. This can mean making some jarring changes to your schedule; you might find yourself getting up at four o'clock each morning so you have two hours to paint or ride the stationary bike. But if you love it, you'll find a way to do it.

The second rule is that you have to be accountable to someone or something that gives you no choice but to do the work. That's the value of a personal trainer. A trainer is someone who will nag you into hitting the weights, give you deadlines, and set up rewards that you can enjoy only after you reach a goal. Invite your best buddy to come by your house at 5:00 A.M. and drag you out of bed and to the gym in your jammies (believe me, most of my buddies would be *delighted* to do this). Make it impossibly hard *not* to follow through. Best of all, have a purpose behind what you do. If you have a cause to motivate you to get out of bed and do what you need to do, you won't need anyone else bugging you.

As I write this, I'm in a constant state of training for one event after another. Following the 2009 Ultraman Canada, I took less than a week off to recover and give my mind a break, but then it was back into the lab and back to work to prepare for the 2009 Ironman World Championship in less than nine weeks. But that's me. It's what I love, and it's what God called me to do.

Back in 2006 I made a sign that said THE LAB and put it above the door of my little condo in Kona. I knew that I needed to structure my life in such a way that training, fitness, and health would become my lifestyle. Today I've made my lifestyle one big Laboratory. The people in my life are all living the same lifestyle, doing what I do, training like I train. I'm surrounded by my Laboratory, and that makes it easy for me to keep my eyes on my goals.

I can't think of a better way to live than being physically fit through swimming, biking, and running. In the end, I still have friends. I still see my daughter. I still go out once in a while. I have a life. It's just centered on my racing, and everyone in my life knows that. My sport is my lifestyle. I've made the rules, and the people I love and trust respect those rules. There's no reason you can't have the same thing.

4

GOD CREATES A LEADER, THEN THE TEAM

"A leader has the vision and conviction that a dream can be achieved. He inspires the power and energy to get it done."
—**Ralph Nader**

When I moved to Hawaii permanently in late 2005, I couldn't swim fifty yards without gasping for air. That might sound surprising considering I had been running marathons and competing in biathlons, but swimming makes completely different aerobic demands on your body. Swimming burns more energy per meter than just about any other form of exercise because not only are you working to gain distance but you're also fighting the resistance of the water. I am doing all that with only one arm. When I started swimming in 2006, I was in for a challenge.

But by this time I had committed to being a triathlete. I had sold my things in California, closed down my art gallery, and, most important, signed up for the Ironman in Arizona. I wasn't going to back out at the first sign of difficulty. I knew that one way or another, I needed to find a coach who was willing to help me in spite of my unique physical situation. I needed a small miracle. I decided to trust God and see what would happen.

After I'd been in Kona all of two days, I went down to the Big Island Running Store to look at some shoes. By the cash register was a little postcard that said, Swimming Lessons: Masters Record Holder Karlyn Pipes-Neilsen. I turned to a guy nearby and said, "Do you know this woman?" He replied, "She's my wife." He pointed to an article on the wall detailing her win in a local swim. Turns out she was a Kona resident and a Masters world champion in swimming. "How can I meet her?" I asked.

The guy, Eric Neilsen, told me that she worked at the store and would be in that night. I got chills. This was God at work. I'd left my coaching situation in his hands, and he had guided me to this person. I talked with Eric for a while about his training for the Boston Marathon, thanked him, and left. When I came back that evening, I asked the woman there if she was Karlyn Pipes-Neilsen and got a huge smile in return. I told her that I was training for the Arizona Ironman in 2007, and I said, "I've never done a triathlon, especially an Ironman, and I can't swim twenty-five yards. Would you train me?" She said, "Let's do it!" We talked about some workout routines, and at the end of the conversation I dropped the bomb. "I have the use of only one arm."

I had no idea if she would laugh at me, tell me I was

crazy, or just walk away. She didn't do any of those things. She looked at me, grinned, and said, "We have a lot of work to do. Meet me at the pool Wednesday."

I showed up at the pool wearing surf shorts. Whoops. I was a runner and a cyclist and superskinny; I was too self-conscious to wear Speedos or spandex, so I wore what I had. Karlyn showed up, saw what I was wearing, and cracked up. Then we got to work. I got in the pool and started doing twenty-five-yard drills. I could barely make it to the other side of the pool. Turns out that surf shorts, because they're baggy, create lots of drag when you're swimming. That was lesson number one. Karlyn told me to come back Friday wearing spandex jammers. I did as I was told.

Over the weeks, as I learned what it meant to train for an Ironman, Karlyn and I developed a wonderful relationship. She cared about me as a person, not as just another client. I think, after all she had accomplished, that I represented a new challenge for her. And I needed someone like that on my team because swimming is my most challenging sport. So three times a week she pushed and encouraged me. In a few weeks I went from swimming five hundred yards a day to swimming one thousand yards a day. I also worked with Eric to refine my running and cycling technique. He taught me how to conserve energy and make the most of my endurance.

Next, Karlyn dropped me into the ocean off the famous Kailua-Kona Pier, where the Ironman World Championship starts. We worked on technique, but mostly we worked on staying afloat. I wasn't comfortable being in the open ocean, and I burned way too much energy trying to keep myself from sinking, which I was sure I was going to do. But she helped me calm down, and over the next three months we got my ocean swimming down pat.

It was just a few weeks before the Arizona Ironman, and I was now swimming up to four thousand yards a day. With Karlyn helping me every step of the way, I had developed a hybrid freestyle stroke that allowed me to use my legs for propulsion while getting the maximum power out of my left arm. I said to her, "At the Ironman, I'm going to get out of the water in two hours." She shook her head. "No, you're going to get out of the water in an hour and a half." On the day of the race, I exited the water at 1:29:29. I should have known better than to doubt Karlyn.

She and Eric were always pushing me, building me up and cheering me on from the very beginning. Karlyn was overwhelmingly positive, which helped me get over my insecurities about swimming. She would bring other coaches over to watch me swim and tell them all about her student with one paralyzed arm and how wonderfully he was doing. My confidence soared. Even with God showing me the way, I couldn't have done what I did without Karlyn and Eric. They were two of the most important members of my team. I truly believe that God sent them to me as angels.

• • •

When I talk about my team, it includes everyone who has helped me prepare for my races and reach the point I'm at today. I'm still amazed at the way that, once I decided that I wanted to become an Ironman and I handed things over to God, people appeared who could help me reach my goals.

I've been blessed with coaches like Karlyn, Eric, and Dave, whom I met at the Western Australia Ironman 2007. I've been lucky enough to have nutritionists, chiropractors, massage therapists, equipment specialists, trainers, and sponsors come into my life at the right time to push me farther along this road.

But my team is even bigger. It's made up of all the people I know and love and who give me their total support. My team goes all the way back to high school. That's where my freshman chemistry teacher, Jerry Marfe, introduced me to the sport of triathlon and the Ironman distance event. He was a pro triathlete who inspired me to start competing in endurance races. I used to watch him working on the indoor bike and doing countless laps around the track. Little did he know he was inspiring a fourteen-year-old boy to become an Ironman twenty years later! Jerry was there to see me finish the Ironman in Arizona, and it's possible I never would have been there without him.

The entire town of Kailua-Kona is my team, too. When I'm racing, I feel like I'm representing my friends and my adopted hometown before the world. In return, the people of Kona have humbled me with a flood of love, support, and kindness. To run the races I've run in my hometown and hear those cheers—it's no exaggeration to say that the people of Kona have taken more than a few seconds off my times due to pure adrenaline.

My experience with all these people led me to realize another truth: **God creates a leader, then the team.**

Let me say right off that I'm no visionary leader. When I made the decision to turn my back on my past life and race the world's most extreme races, I didn't know what I was doing. I only knew that God had given me a vision of what I could accomplish in his name, and I had to pursue it. What makes someone a leader is the vision, not a need for power. If you open your mind and your heart to God and let him place in you a purpose larger than yourself, and if you accept that purpose without reservation, people will appear in your life to help you achieve that goal. We all need other people to help us reach the Promised Land.

I certainly did. When I decided to become an Ironman, I was a raw distance athlete lacking in technique and strategy. I didn't know how to eat, train, or prepare for the challenges of a race. All I had going for me was a stubborn will that refused to quit and a white-hot passion to do this. But in what was surely a miracle, people like Karlyn and Eric began to appear and provide the support, positive energy, and expert guidance that I needed if I was going to finish an Ironman, much less an Ultraman.

In our society, we're very proud of being rugged individuals who can do things on our own. We insist that we don't need anyone's help. In fact, we regard asking for help as a sign of weakness. But that's all an illusion. The truth is that we've always depended on one another. Nothing truly worthwhile ever happens because of one individual alone. In recent years we've moved away from that sense of depending on each other because of things like television and the Internet, which allow us to isolate ourselves. But we still need each other. We're so much stronger when we combine our knowledge, vision, and purpose.

This book wouldn't exist without my agent and editors

and many other people who made it a reality. I would not have won the ESPY without thousands of people taking the time to vote for me. I couldn't have finished Ultraman or any of my other races without dozens of people supporting me. By myself, I'm just a man who can swim, cycle, and run far. But with my team by my side, I'm *unstoppable*.

If there's something that you're dying to do or achieve, one of the best things you can do is surrender yourself to your dream. Let yourself radiate joy and passion . . . because God put them there. That's how you know you're on the right path. Stop trying to be an island. Don't set out to learn and do everything on your own. Be open to others who appear in your life with skills or knowledge you need—because they will appear. It's amazing how soon and suddenly the team starts to come together. Listen to other people who can help you, and embrace what they offer. Then instead of an island, you become like a tree trunk—at the center of the system but dependent on all the other parts.

If you want to start a business, get your spouse to help out. If you're trying to lose weight and get fit, work out with your kids in the room, or have them ride their bikes with you while you run. Make your closest friends part of a special project, or just ask their opinions. Find those people who you know will never doubt you, and integrate them in some way into your vision. When you eventually succeed, they will feel that they had some small role to play in your triumph, and that's a fantastic feeling to have.

When you can do that, you're inspiring other people at the same time that you're getting closer and closer to the goals God has in mind for you. You're enriching other lives while blessing your own. What a way to live! It doesn't get much better than that.

I've been fortunate enough to get to know some really incredible people during this journey, none more important to me than my coach, Dave Ciaverella. I met Dave in 2007 when I was racing the Western Australia Ironman; he and his wife, Ann, were racing there and I sat with them at the awards banquet the night after the race. It turned out that Ann had won her age group and set a course record while Dave nearly broke nine hours. I thought, *Wow, what a couple of badasses.* But I didn't know Dave was a coach.

When I saw them the next day on the bus back to Perth, I found out a lot more about Dave: he was a neuroradiologist who still worked sixty hours a week as a doctor while training for Ironman races, and (this still blows me away) he had taken eighteenth place in the national Men's Marathon Championships in 1995 *while he was still in medical school.* The guy was killing himself in classes all day, then running one hundred miles every week. But while he had informally coached some athletes, the only person he coached full-time for Ironman was Ann. He didn't feel he had the time. But he gave me his card and told me to look him up if I was in Portland, Oregon.

I headed off to race in Canada, and I had a terrible race. I immediately called Dave and said, "I need to train and I need you to help me." He said, "Come to Portland." So I hopped on a plane in Vancouver, flew to Oregon, and ended up staying with Dave and Ann for a month. It wasn't like a coach-student relationship; it was more like a brotherhood. Dave instantly became the most vital part of my team.

I found out that he had a different way of training triathletes. A lot of coaches want you to be out training all day long; Dave was into more fast-paced, short training. I thrived on it. After a short time training with him, I could feel myself not only becoming stronger, but also developing more confidence. I wasn't sure if my times would improve with Dave, but that didn't matter as much as having greater consistency and a stronger mental game.

Where Dave has really become my anchor is in his attitude toward my goals. He's one of the few people I've ever met who is as passionate and driven as I am. So in the beginning of 2008, when I told him that I wanted to do Ultraman, his only response was "We need to put a plan together. You follow my plan, and you'll get to the finish line." He'd never coached an Ultraman athlete before, but he knew exactly what to do for me. When I had told other coaches about my Ultraman aspirations, they told me I might want to reevaluate my goals. Their first reaction was doubt that I could achieve what I wanted; Dave's reaction was that he was going to give me the tools to succeed and the rest was up to me. I am forever grateful to him for that.

Dave's incredible: a former state high-school cross-country champion who still dominates his age group in triathlons despite working long hours every week in a level-one trauma center. He can whip every one of his students in a race, but instead he really likes to see people succeed. He teaches us to compete with him, to kick his butt. The guy who didn't have time to coach now has about twenty-six athletes he's coaching, and they all love him. What also blows me away is that he knows how broke a lot of triathletes are, so he charges a fraction of what other elite coaches typically charge. His generosity is incredible, and his results are, too: in 2009, twenty-two of his athletes set personal records in Ironman races.

What makes Dave the perfect coach for me is that, like me, he has no limits. When I see something, I have a vision and I go after it. Dave is the same way. He's passionate about his athletes, but he doesn't talk about it much so when he does express his pride, it means a lot more. When I was nominated for the ESPY in 2009, I invited Dave to come to Los Angeles for the awards. He flew in the night before. We were in the hotel kicking back, and after a while he turned to me and said, with tears in his eyes, "I am so proud of you. In all my racing and coaching, this is the highlight."

I don't think there's a better way an athlete can honor his coach than by kicking butt. Dave is in my head before and during every race—encouraging me, driving me, letting me know he believes in me. In fact, I can honestly say he's the only person in my racing life I am certain has never doubted what I could do. His coaching is about me being the best athlete I can possibly be. I don't think I could have gone to the starting line of my first Ultraman without his voice in my ear. Even when I got stung by the jellyfish and had to be hauled into the rescue boat, it was Dave's voice I heard challenging me, saying, "This is how you're going to go out?" It was me not wanting to let down him, or God, that got me back into the water.

At the end of the day, all I really need is someone who knows what I'm capable of and says, "We have work to do, here's your plan for tomorrow." That's Dave. God has never given me a greater blessing than to make this man—this doctor, world-class athlete, and teacher—my coach and guide.

I'm on a journey of self-discovery, and as time goes on I'm discovering something amazing: you can be the leader of a team and at the same time be a part of someone else's team. None of us is on top in every aspect of life. The guy who's an elite triathlete on the weekends might be a dedicated dad helping out in his child's classroom on weekday mornings. The lawyer who schools people in the courtroom could be a foot soldier for her church's fund-raising efforts on the weekends. We all have the potential to be visionary leaders, and we all have the responsibility to help others realize their visions.

That's one of the reasons I created the Never Stop Foundation. Much of the money I raise with my projects—books, movies, speaking, charity events—goes to the foundation. The foundation's mission is to build the Never Stop Performance Center in Kailua-Kona in 2012. The NSPC will be a training and learning center where young people and adults will find the support and resources they need to build better physical, mental, and spiritual lives through athletics. The project is gaining support and moving closer to fruition.

I want to use athletics to teach young people how to think creatively about their lives and help them develop the practical skills to turn their dreams into reality, whether they dream about competing in triathlons or going to graduate school. The Never Stop Foundation is my way of becoming part of the team for a lot of other people who may have grown up like I did.

When I challenge myself in the extreme races to come, I will depend even more on the support and love of my team—the people who have been selfless enough to dedicate their time, energy, and knowledge to helping me reach for my dreams. None of us achieves anything alone. No matter how talented or independent you think you are, you're never going to get to the finish line on your own. Behind each of us is a team waiting to come together.

5

YOU VERSUS YOU

"The spirit, the will to win, and the will to excel are the things that endure. These qualities are so much more important than the events that occur."
—**Vince Lombardi**

The race started at 7:00 A.M., and I had a fantastic swim through the warm waters of Puako Bay even though the swim portion of any triathlon is always my greatest challenge. I swam in a long rectangle parallel to the shore, turned clockwise at the buoys, and kept pace with the other athletes. I made a right turn at the final buoy and hit the shore right at the time I had told my coach I would be out of the water. I felt awesome as I ran across the timing mats to the parking lot that was the staging area for the cycling portion of the race.

As I climbed on my bike, I told myself that for the next fifty-six miles I was going to put my head down and hammer as hard as I could up to the town of Hawi and back. I was willing to blow up or bonk in order to keep up with the competition. But I was confident heading into what I knew was my strength.

Along with the other more than 1,100 competitors who would eventually finish, I cruised onto Queen Ka'ahumanu Highway and then onto Akoni Pule Highway, the "road to Hawi," the roughest part of the climb. It was about 90 degrees and humid—typical May weather on the Big Island. As the ride progressed, I kept getting stronger and stronger. I found myself on the left side of the shoulder, passing what seemed to be pack after pack of bikers. Most didn't notice; they were locked into the intense concentration that comes with the pain and mental pressure of a triathlon. But as I shot by them on uphill stretches, some turned their heads in surprise as if to say, "What the heck was that?" Even I was wondering, *What's going on here?*

I scorched past the aid stations and hit the dismount area to begin the run stage, feeling strong, strong, strong. I felt that effortless rush, like God was letting me draft off him, adding speed by picking up on his tailwind. Then I got off the bike—and the energy drained from my legs like somebody had yanked a plug from the base of my spine. My quads were tight, my calves hated me, and it felt like it was 150 degrees outside. Whoa. I hadn't expected this, and I seriously wondered if I had blown myself up on the bike course. I had a thirteen-mile run ahead of me, half of which would be on a humid golf course with rolling hills, but I honestly didn't know if my body was going to be able to come out of the bonk stage. I was overheating.

• • •

It was May 30, 2009. The race was the Ironman 70.3 Hawaii, also known as the Honu 70.3. The Honu (Hawaiian for "turtle") 70.3 is one of the hardest yet most beautiful half-Ironman races in the 70.3 Ironman series. Honu is a big deal for Hawaii residents because it's a qualifying event for the Ironman World Championship, the Super Bowl of all Ironmans.

I had competed in the Ironman World Championship in 2008, but as you'll recall, I'd gotten in through a competitor lottery. This year I was aiming at a new goal. I wanted to qualify for the Ironman World Championship on my own merit. To do that, I had to finish in the top three in my age group in the Big Island resident category—not against other challenged athletes, but *against able-bodied athletes.* No shortcuts allowed.

The funny thing was I knew half the guys I would be racing against to qualify for Ironman. I had seen them out on the road and talked strategy, training tips, and local gossip with them on a regular basis. They were all good guys the other 364 days of the year. But not today. Today they were barriers to jump over. I wanted to swim, cycle, and run them into the ground.

You go into a challenge like this as confident and prepared as you possibly can be, but at the same time, you have to be realistic. I didn't set my sights on winning the Honu. My goal was to beat at least six other Big Island residents in the thirty-five to thirty-nine age group. To make that happen, months ahead of time I analyzed the race like a science experiment. I knew that half of the other guys in my category had raced the previous year, and a couple of them had raced the past four years, so I got their times in each stage and broke the numbers down.

I sat down with my coach, Dave, and gave him the numbers—when I needed to be out of the water, when I had to be off the bike. Based on my previous times, I had to make some improvement, so we went to work. Knowing that running is my strength, I had to shave some time off my swim and my ride.

This would be the first race in which I was competing to place and the first time I was trying to qualify for an event. The pressure was on.

● ● ●

Once I climbed off my bike, it was a struggle to get my legs moving into a run. The humidity was through the roof, and so was my core temperature. My feet felt like they were sinking into the turf. I thought, *This is going to be a long thirteen miles.* After a few miles I had found a rhythm but couldn't stop feeling dehydrated even though I was drinking cup after cup of water and Gatorade at every aid station. It was *hot.* Would the heat kill my chance at qualifying for Ironman? It was like running through a sauna. The heat was dangerous; high humidity prevents the body from perspiring and cooling itself, so if you're not careful you can run right past uncomfortable and into heat exhaustion.

This was torture. I was feeling weak, but God spoke to me and reminded me, "Jason, take a look around." I did, and I saw that all the other athletes were struggling, too.

Everybody felt the heat. Nobody had an advantage. I quit worrying and just focused on putting one foot in front of the other.

As I approached mile four I had to pass two other guys, and right at mile four I slid into fourth place in my division. But the guy in third place had qualified in previous years, and I knew I had my work cut out for me if I was going to catch him. The way the run course was set up, there were a couple of out-and-backs (courses that loop around on themselves) so you could see who was in front of you running in the opposite direction. At about mile eight, when I saw the guy in third place, I couldn't help but be discouraged. *I have nothing in the tank,* I thought. *I'm simply racing to survive.*

But I kept going. One foot in front of the other. More ice down my pants. More water over my head. My shoes seemed to weigh about fifty pounds each. But I wanted this. I had visualized it in training. I felt myself crossing the finish line and qualifying for Ironman. I had put in the work and knew that God had my back. I had nothing to prove to anybody but myself: that I would race the 2009 Ironman World Championship as a qualified athlete. In the last three miles, I shifted my racing strategy. I simply gave it everything I had. I stopped drinking from the aid station. I stopped grabbing for ice and water and started to run out of fear that I had blown my chance. The next thing I knew, I was running right behind the guy in third place. Then I passed him. I was in third place.

I kept telling myself, *Stay relaxed, don't become overconfident, run your race.* Then it was prayer time. *God,* I began, *you showed me a vision. Come with me these final miles, be my source of inspiration and energy, and bring me to the finish line.* In a flash, I felt like I had started sprinting. Thoughts of being dehydrated or in pain vanished. Then I could hear the race announcer from a distance, and I knew that the race had now just begun. I've said this before and I'll say it again: training and racing are 20 percent physical and 80 percent mental. As long as you rely on training and natural ability and will to compete, you're tapping only part of the mental energy that God gives us all. But as soon as you rely completely on God, that energy becomes 100 percent pure, and you're capable of pushing beyond your limits. Those last three miles, God gave me the strength to pump my legs; I just hung on.

I started to visualize the finish. I could see more fans out on the course and knew that the finish line was less than a mile away. My final thoughts were, *Throw all your cards on the table, and give it all you have.* I knew the guy I had just passed might be right on my heels; he could pass me and knock me out of qualifying. So I began to sprint. This race was mine. I wasn't going to let anyone take it from me. As I ran down the finishers' chute with people screaming my name, I looked up to the sky and blew a kiss to God and said, *Through Christ, all things are possible.*

I crossed the finish line in third place in my age group, finishing the race in 5:43:27. Out of 1,100 competitors, I finished 353rd. A horde of friends and well-wishers rushed up, but all I could do was praise God and thank him. I almost fell to my knees right there.

• • •

Some people believe in an angry, punishing God. I don't. From everything I have experienced, God is not easy to serve, and sometimes his will can be completely confusing, but he always has your back. I believe in God, but I know also that he believes in me. When things are dark in my life, that's what I know I can rely on.

So if God isn't throwing up obstacles as we try to climb our personal mountains and run life's endurance races, who is? I think it's us. We're often our own worst enemies. Look at me: all through high school and then at Arizona State University I had a clear path as an endurance athlete laid out before me, but what did I do instead? I went to Los Angeles to work for a sports marketing firm. I took a detour to Hollywood.

What you read about the Hollywood lifestyle is the truth. It's addictive. Who you know, who you hang out with, and where you work all seem to be the only things that matter. After working hard all day, people would go relax at one of the hangouts where A-list stars rub elbows with professional athletes. I soon found myself entangled in a web of drugs and alcohol, buying into the belief that "the harder you work, the harder you play." Soon the lifestyle started taking a toll on my career as well as on my relationships.

Back then I was seeking happiness. I thought the more hours I worked and the more money I made, the more I would enjoy life. I was wrong. I was lost and seeking truth. Sometimes, in seeking the truth, you take wrong turns. But are they really wrong? Or does God allow us to go down a foolish path to mold us, make us wiser, and shape our character? I did drugs. I struggled with addiction. I think I abused Ecstasy because I liked the way it made me feel: free, accepted, loved, and cared for—everything I missed as a child.

After my dad passed away I didn't have a role model. Not once did I have to bring home a report card and show it to my parents. I had to teach myself right and wrong. I mostly raised myself, especially when I was on my own at age seventeen, and I failed over and over in doing it. But I honestly wouldn't have it any other way. My experiences helped mold me into the man I am today. If I had not gone through such a time of being lost, I wouldn't be able to talk about God and hope to people who have experienced their own pain and suffering. God allowed me to go down these paths and also led me into the light.

The point is sometimes we just can't get out of our own way. Whether the goal is to climb Mount Everest, start a business, or just graduate from high school, human beings are incredibly efficient at listening to the wrong voices. To one person, the inner voice whispers, "It's too risky; stay here where it's comfortable." To someone else, the voice mutters, "No, you'd rather have that temporary pleasure over there than put in years of work and sacrifice, wouldn't you?" And of course, there's always that devil on our shoulders hissing the worst one of all: "You're not good enough."

What stops you from having the life you dream about is not your job, your friends, or the economy. Your real competition is found elsewhere. In the race of life, **it's you versus you.**

Our flesh and spirit are always battling each other. Spirit drives us to listen to God and walk in step with him, but flesh drives us to argue with others, get distracted, ignore signs from God, and make stupid decisions. The trick is learning to balance the two and knowing when to let spirit guide us. Sometimes listening to the flesh is smart, especially when your body is telling you that you need rest, peace, fuel, or exercise. But when it comes to the bigger picture, spirit knows what the flesh can't comprehend. Only in spirit do we tap into the resources that make us unstoppable. Spirit was what enabled me to run those last three miles of the Honu 70.3 when I had nothing left in my tank.

But it's easy to ignore spirit. So we make bad choices. We go for the quick buzz instead of making the sacrifice that's going to pay off in the long run—buying the $50,000 car instead of the $20,000 model so we can save the rest for a down payment on a house. We quit because we fear failure. Instead of looking at failure as God's great teacher, we view it as a judgment. *If I fail, that means I don't have what it takes.* If triathletes did that, there wouldn't be any triathletes! There's hardly a racer out there who hasn't failed at a race. The ones who are up the next morning back in the training routine are the ones who become respected, successful competitors.

• • •

In a way, I like it when the cards are stacked against me. It's motivating. Heck, the deck has been stacked against me my entire life. Since I was twelve, people have asked me, "How are you possibly going to play baseball with one arm? How do you even tie your shoes?" But I never asked those questions; I just went out and did it.

Today, when people gasp, "How on earth do you swim six miles with one arm?" I just shrug. Sometimes I don't know. I believe in God and myself, and I just do it.

Part of the key for me is that I've never looked at myself as being disabled. I have a physical challenge, but we all have some kind of challenge. Some people have bad knees or rotten eyesight or back pain. Others have challenges that aren't physical but just as real, from phobias and anxiety to the conviction that they're not worthy. If you give in to negative thinking, you give yourself an excuse for quitting: "I did my best, but you see, I have this arm, and . . ." Instead, you can choose to see your challenges as hurdles that will make you stronger as you clear them. I've chosen to manage my paralyzed arm as just one more challenge on the road to my goals.

In the battle of you versus you, it's vital to put yourself in a position to succeed. The flesh always tempts us and tries to drown out the higher self, our spirit, by offering come-ons like a used car salesman. Ice cream left in the freezer seduces dieters while people trying to pay off credit card debt are led astray by sales and department store windows. To give spirit the best chance to win, you've got to minimize the flesh's opportunities.

That's why I've chosen to live in Hawaii. It's secluded. It's like a camp with everything I need to be successful: warm weather, beautiful water, endless roads to ride, and by far the best fans in the world. I made a decision to set up my life in such a way that racing would be my lifestyle. I set up my Laboratory, knowing there were things in my life I had to sacrifice. In Kona, when the sun goes down, the lights are out for me. Then the sun comes up, and I know what my purpose is. I thank God for giving me another day and another opportunity to train the body he gave me to be in the best shape possible.

In the end, there's no difference between you and someone like Bill Gates. There's only the ability to set aside what the flesh is clamoring for in favor of what spirit wants you to achieve. The flesh always wants the same things: short-term pleasure, comfort, and the easy way out, all with minimal effort. The flesh doesn't think about the long term or the broader vision; it's our baser nature, the part that wants what it wants now. It's the adolescent part of ourselves—all about hormones and acting on every impulse.

Spirit is about maturity. It's about delayed gratification. It's about taking the long view and sacrificing pleasure in the moment so that you can enjoy something far greater down the line. Spirit is what makes us invest for a prosperous retirement and put something away for our kids' college tuition. It convinces us to quit a good job to start our own business even though we know that means two years of working eighty-hour weeks and just scraping by. Choosing spirit means getting up every morning at five to run or spending every spare hour doing research for the book you want to write. Spirit means loving the process as much as the goal, the journey as much as the finish. It's about knowing that you're following the path God has laid out for you and finding joy in each stage no matter how tough it is.

Being guided by the wisdom of spirit is what makes people great. Vision, hard work, sacrifice, and belief in oneself over the long term are the recipe for incredible achievements. Every great triathlete I know could have chosen at any point to listen to the flesh and say, "This is too much pain. I'm not going to train today." But if you do that too often, you trade your long-term dream for a little short-term relief, and to me that's a bad bargain. The great ones in any field—sports, business, politics, the arts—care more about their future than about anything that tempts them today. Lead me not into temptation? That's absolutely right.

• • •

So what do you care about enough to sacrifice for? Knowing the answer to that question and following your big-picture vision are the keys to living the life you want—the life God wants for you. But be sure to do it in your own way. My road is mine because it works for me. I'm an extreme guy. I can't give myself the opportunity to be tempted by anything because I won't risk getting pulled away from my athletic goals. But you don't have to do it the same way.

The first key to winning the "you versus you" battle is to know what you want so badly that you'll give up what makes you feel comforted today. You've got to be ready to exchange that for what will make you feel exhilarated, fulfilled, and at one with God five years from now—and then for the rest of your life. Your passion must be some irresistible desire that God has placed in you that can't be ignored. It may emerge through unusual circumstances, like my witnessing my first Ironman in 2004, but it will emerge. When it does, pay attention. Don't dismiss it as too hard or inconvenient, and don't say no because you worry about what other people will think of you. The only opinion that matters is the one that God has of you.

The second key is to know how to listen to your flesh and spirit and tell one from the other. Your flesh will always tell you to do what is easy, what you're used to, and what doesn't challenge your beliefs. But if you listen to flesh, how will you grow as a person? You probably won't. You'll stagnate. Your spirit will encourage you to do the things that are difficult, make you nervous, and deny you the pleasures that you may have loved in the past. For instance, if you're trying to get in the best physical shape of your life, you'll need to eat a healthy diet. But when you come home from the gym for lunch, flesh and spirit will fight. Flesh doesn't care if you torpedo the great workout you just did by eating a cheeseburger and fries; spirit will nudge you toward the salmon and brown rice. When you recognize the flesh as the voice that will lead you off course and away from your goal, you'll be better able to ignore it.

The third key to success is starting small. When you do, it's easier to achieve some early successes that will carry you to the next level. Try to do too much too fast, and you set yourself up for failure. Your flesh will say, "See? I told you this was too hard," and you will give up before you ever really start. I didn't begin by competing in an Ironman distance event. I spent years running 5Ks, 10Ks, half-marathons, marathons, and biathlons. Then I got interested in competing in the Ironman distance. Sometimes it seems like I've been training for the Ironman for the past twenty years.

God's belief in us is never in question; he knows what we can achieve. It's our own belief that needs work. With each success, whether it's losing five pounds on the way to fifty or finishing a renovation project on your home, your belief will soar.

The fourth key is something I learned in my Honu 70.3 race: stay humble. Remember, I got overconfident about my abilities on the bike and almost burned myself out for the run. So now when I race I don't let my mind run off toward overconfidence. I focus on getting from point A to point B. I keep myself humble by communing with God and reminding myself that everything I have I owe to him. I don't put myself in a position to be tempted by overconfidence. That's also why I have such a strict training regimen that hardly allows me any flexibility in scheduling runs, bikes, and swims and in planning what I eat. I limit my options so I don't get arrogant about my willpower. Forget willpower. I'd rather have humility and preparation.

The fifth and final key is to accept that listening to spirit isn't easy. When you give up on quick-fix pleasures to pursue a bigger vision, there's going to be work. You'll probably feel some pain and fear, and at times you'll want desperately to give up. Think about how hard entrepreneurs work to launch companies, putting in endless hours and going months without knowing how they'll make payroll. But they do it because they have a dream that in a few years they'll have a thriving business that will allow them to live the life that they know God wants for them.

So many books and seminars and CDs insist that change is easy and following your dreams is as simple as saying affirmations when you get up in the morning. That's just not true. Discovering all the incredible things God has in store for you *is* as easy as opening your mind and heart to him, that's true. But making your dreams a reality will always take work and sacrifice. Don't buy into the lie that change is easy, or you'll give up quickly. Instead, embrace the work. Learn to love the hardship; it will make you a better, stronger person.

You don't have to go to extremes to follow your spirit. You can incorporate your calling into some parts of your life instead of the whole thing. But be aware that a kind of "survival of the fittest" selection process goes to work here. When you pursue your spirit-driven goal, the parts of your life that are healthy will fit with that goal. The parts that are unhealthy will not, and they will probably fall away. So if your job consumes so much of your life that it leaves you no time or energy to work on your dream, you'll probably end up finding another job. Same for friends: the ones who encourage and support you will stick around while the ones who feed you negative thoughts will be gone. You'll make big changes in your life when your spirit is in control.

My spirit compels me to constantly push the outer edge of my endurance. That's why I'm coming up with new challenges like doing five Iron-distance triathlons on five islands on five consecutive days. I can't rest on my laurels. I don't want to become complacent because then I lose the thing that got me where I am today: the knowledge that my mind and will can push me beyond any reasonable limits to get to the finish line. God commanded me to keep taking risks and believing in his purpose for me. That means being willing to live on the edge. Part of my "you versus you" battle is not giving in to the desire to sit back and congratulate myself.

Don't get me wrong: after you have struggled and sacrificed to fulfill God's vision, you need to stop and savor what you've accomplished. A healthy bit of pride feeds your faith in yourself. By all means, take pleasure in reaching your goals. But make sure you cross the finish line before you start celebrating. Don't push yourself so hard in the cycling stage that you have nothing left for the run. That's a mistake I won't ever make again. Instead, keep putting out consistent effort and moving toward that big dream. Because, believe me, when you get there after working and sweating and trusting God, there is nothing better.

6

GOD'S GOT YOUR BACK

"God sends a cross, but He also sends the strength to bear it."
—**Leo Tolstoy**

I was crying my eyes out and I shouldn't have been. I was making my way to the starting line of the 2008 Ultraman World Championship, the race I'd had my eye on for two years. This was the culmination of a dream for me, the reward for endless hours of pounding the roads and hitting the bike and hammering lap after lap in the pool. I should have been feeling joyful and grateful to God, but I wasn't. In reality, I felt alone. Lost. Like nobody had my back.

For one thing, I was tired. After the 2008 Ironman World Championship in Kona the month before, I was wiped out. It was my mind more than my body that was tired. I had either raced or trained nonstop for ten months, and I needed a break. Instead, after only one day off following the Ironman, I resumed training. Unlike most Ironman athletes, who finish their season with the Ironman World Championship, then go home and rest up during November and December, I couldn't afford time off. I still had a huge race left, and I was having a rough time getting my head into it.

I had temporarily cut off most contact with my friends and family because I knew I needed to be alone to focus. I let one person—Dave, my coach—into my world as much as I could. He needed to know how I was feeling, but I didn't tell him that I was spent. I remember lying on the couch in my rented apartment in Portland, where I had gone to train with Dave for a couple months, and thinking, *I can't do another day of this, getting up early, training three sessions a day.* I wasn't inspired. I was beat up, and I missed my friends and family. I missed having a social life. I felt like I was in prison.

I knew what I needed. I called Dave and told him I was going back to Hawaii. I needed to be there. I wanted to feel the heat, have the island beneath my feet, and be around the area where I would race. Just the thought of being back in Hawaii got me stoked. I landed and it was hot. I needed that heat because the race would be hot.

The day of the race I was up at 3:30 in the morning, consuming high-calorie carbohydrate drink to ensure that my muscles stored every possible molecule of fuel (a process called "topping off"). Then my friends and crew members Doug and Annette accompanied me down to the pier where the race would begin. That was when I started to get emotional. It all hit me hard—everything I had gone through to get to this point, everything I had lost and sacrificed to follow my dream. I suddenly missed my father more than I had since the day he died. I wished that he could be there so I could say, "Dad, look, I became an athlete after all, thanks to you!"

I missed my little girl, Katana, whom I'd hardly seen while I was training for Ironman and Ultraman. I mourned the lost time with her that I would never get back, and I cried wishing that she could be there so she could be proud of her daddy. I couldn't help thinking about all the people I had lost in my life and how I wanted them there for support. It was selfish that I wanted them there for myself, but there you go. I couldn't feel God with me. I felt alone and lost, and for a second I didn't really understand the purpose of him bringing me there.

Then, thankfully, we began moving toward the start. As I watched Bree and Doug put Bree's kayak in the water, I started to think, *Is this really happening? Am I really here getting ready to race the Ultraman?* I was surrounded by elite endurance athletes. I was struck that God would use as his instrument the kid who seemed to have lost everything but gained the world. I put all my emotions to the side, looked across the bay as far as I could see, and told myself, *Get from point A to point B within the next six hours.* I focused on the facts: this was my calling, I had put in the training, and there was no reason I couldn't go the distance.

Then it struck me. I wasn't alone. I wasn't lost. I was right where I was supposed to be. I had become used to nobody having my back, everyone doubting me. But that was in the past. What got me through my sadness at that moment was the incredible love and support that I felt from all the people who were there on my team that day. I had talked to Dave before the start. He'd said to me, "You have no worries. I know that you can do this." Dave knew I could finish; so did Bree and Doug and Annette and my friends from Kona who had gotten up early to be there for the start. I needed to be able to lean on them because for the past year I'd been struggling. I wasn't sure if anybody else around me really had my back.

For the entire year I'd been training, when I told people that I was going to race and finish the Ultraman World Championship, I felt their doubts. Even friends and other athletes who had seen me race and knew what I could do raised their eyebrows when I told them about my plans. This can be a deeply ego-driven sport, and sometimes it's hard for other triathletes to give more than just a "good for you" to someone who might be competing against them a few months later. I understand that, but grudging encouragement is one thing; obvious disbelief is another.

Nobody doubted my running or biking ability. But swimming 6.2 miles with my one skinny wing? Many didn't think it was possible. A lot of people who really cared about me thought I was deluding myself, setting myself up to fail. I think some of them hoped I would reconsider; after all, hadn't I just completed my first Ironman World Championship a month before? Why would I want to taint that wonderful achievement by getting myself into a race where my likely outcome was failure?

I talk about inspiration a lot. I'm both humbled and proud that God has chosen me to try to inspire even a few people by doing extreme races with a physical challenge. But at the same time, I need inspiration. Anyone who works insanely hard toward a goal does. We all need someone to come along, clap us on the shoulder, and say, "I believe in you!" I didn't get much of that leading up to race day. Those are the times when you have to dig within and inspire yourself.

Then Doug looked at me and said, "Get in." Get in? *Yes, get in. It's time. Let's do this.* I texted Dave, and as I looked down, I saw there were twenty-eight text messages from my friends around the world, all saying basically the same thing: *Jason, you are incredible, and you will crush this race.* I felt the Holy Spirit come upon me. I looked across the waters, the dark skies, and the quiet town of Kona. As soon as my feet touched the water, I could no longer hear anything. I was in the zone. I was ready.

Then came the announcer's voice: "Swimmers, you have sixty seconds to the start of the 2008 Ultraman World Championship!" We all jostled for position, then *boom!* Off we went.

I was finally at peace. The hours upon hours I had spent in the pool, the thousands of miles I had biked and hundreds of hours I had spent pounding the pavement during the past twelve months were all going to work for me over the next thirty-two hours. Those thoughts consumed me, and before I knew it we were past the two-mile marker even though it felt like the gun had just gone off.

• • •

You know the story of that day's swim: jellyfish, jellyfish, and more jellyfish. After surviving that adventure, it was on to the first day of the cycling stage. When I got on my bike to make the trek up to Volcano, I did a mental body check from head to toe. Wow, was I hot. Overheating was an understatement.

I needed to get to Volcano, and I needed to get there fast. I didn't know exactly how much time I had. I just knew I would have to give everything I had to beat the cutoff time. There was no time to waste. When I got to the top of the hill at the town of Kealakekua, I heard a *snap!* Suddenly my bike chain would not move into the big ring, the power ring. That meant I wouldn't have the higher, faster gears available on the downhills, which would cost me speed and time. Another challenge. It was incredibly demoralizing; you can train your body until it's a mile-eating machine, but a simple mechanical glitch can ruin your race . . . or at least make it much harder. I had Doug and Annette radio tech support; they reported that it would be twenty minutes or more before they would arrive. Ticktock, ticktock.

Vern of BikeWorks showed up, and he discovered that my gear cable was snapped off clean, like someone had cut it. Five, then ten minutes went by. He was having trouble rerouting the cable. Finally, I said, "Vern, I have to get to Volcano. I don't have time for this. I'll ride it in my small ring." In minutes I was back on the bike, head down, grinding. I still had no clue how much time I had to get to the finish. I wasn't worried about the time or distance, and now that I look back I'm glad I wasn't. As I said earlier, I made it to Volcano with barely fifteen minutes to spare.

Right after I crossed that day's finish line, I had Doug throw me in the truck and rush us straight to our rented house. I was broken. My legs were spent. I felt like I had spent a day on a battlefield. I lay down on the couch; Doug and Annette fed me carbs, bread and pasta; and I tried to drink as much liquid as possible. I knew I had to be up at 4:00 A.M. to start topping off for the next day, but I wasn't looking forward to that. My legs were throbbing, and I was freezing. Volcano is at 3,700 feet, and it was cold in the rental with no heat. There was one floor heater for the whole house, and Doug and Annette set it in my room so I could have a few hours of comfortable sleep.

But my body wasn't cooperating. I *hurt*. I was dehydrated and having muscle spasms, and my head was pounding. All I wanted was a good night's rest. The clock approached 10:00 P.M., then 11:00, then midnight. I sat and watched it, unable to sleep. *Great,* I thought. *I'm not going to get a wink. How will my body hold up tomorrow?* Then I thought, *Wait, whose race is this? It's not mine.* I quickly went into prayer, and before I knew it my alarm was sounding. I sat up at the end of the bed and slammed my 600 calories of carbs.

I was officially finished with Day One of the Ultraman World Championship, something I had dreamed about for the past year. I could barely believe it. Then thoughts of my daughter, Katana, started to drift in. This sport can be very lonely at times. Spending all those hours isolated in training can wear on your emotions. But come game day, it all makes sense. Katana is one of my biggest sources of inspiration, and just the thought of her always seems to make me stronger. *Katana* means "sword" in Japanese, and she is my protector.

As Day Two started, we rushed to get ready. There is an incredible amount to get accomplished before you can head to the start. My prerace ritual fuel is always the same: 500 to 600 calories of Malto drink premade in a bottle and sipped over the course of thirty minutes. I start to drink my G2 Gatorade about a half hour from the start to top off my sodium levels and fluids, which are vital to my performance and my health.

The start in Volcano was cold; everyone was wearing jackets and long tights. My plan for the day was to be steady and consistent. There is a nineteen-mile descent out of Volcano to the first turn where you head south to the Red Road along the Puna Coast. The leaders of the pack took off like rockets; they must have been going forty miles per hour or more. With twelve hours to complete the 176-mile trek, I was content to cruise at thirty and play it safe.

My crew met me at the bottom of the hill, and right away they started playing cheer squad. Annette would jump around like a cheerleader, and Doug would throw down some break-dance moves. It brought a smile to my face as I set up my game plan for the next 150 miles, which was basically to stay consistent and not blow up. As I approached the Red Road, my team handed me the fuel and water that would carry me over for the next twenty miles; they were not allowed to follow me.

As I passed through Hilo, I thought about Katana. She lives in Hilo with her mother, and I wanted her to come and see me as I raced through. I had Doug call Renee and ask if she could bring my little girl down to the main highway within the hour. No answer. My heart sank.

Otherwise, the day seemed to be going well till I hit the thirteen-mile climb up to the small town of Honokaa. *Crash.* Suddenly I had no energy. I had decided that as part of my race strategy, I would eat anything and everything on this ride in order to fuel up for the fifty-two-mile run on Day Three, and my Carbo Pro was not cutting it. Scones, pizza slices, it all looked the same to me by 150 miles, and I was stuffing it in my mouth as fast as I could swallow. All of a sudden I felt my neck starting to drop, a sure sign of fatigue. I was tired and—quite honestly—I was bored. I wanted this day to be over. Blessedly, massage therapist Dawn Henry showed up, and it was time to get off the bike and on to the tailgate of Doug's truck. Ahhh. Massage time. I had my shoes off, my helmet unstrapped, and I swear I had the best five minutes of massage a human being has ever enjoyed.

Then I yelled, "Let's roll!" and I was back in the saddle with my right hand strapped to the handlebars. Time to battle the beast into the town of Waimea and on to the eight-mile climb up the Kohala Mountains. As soon as I could see the town, it was as though I got a fresh pair of legs. Stage Two was almost in the bag! But as we approached the base of the Kohalas, I could already tell that we were in for a challenging climb. These mountains are notorious for wind, and that day was going to be no exception. With Doug at my back I began climbing: 7 percent grade, 8 percent, 9 percent, 10 percent . . . for the next seven miles. I quickly realized that I had nothing in the tank. I was toast. Doug later told me that on a dangerous six-mile descent with a crosswind, he was worried about my neck dropping and he almost pulled me off my bike a few times. My neck and shoulder muscles were at near failure from holding my bike steady in the wind and that meant I couldn't hold my head up to see where I was going. Biking with one arm for 176 miles and not being able to stand in the saddle on any of the climbs just grinds you down.

As we neared the top of the mountains, I knew we had a nice ten-mile descent. But there was a crosswind of at least thirty miles per hour, so all the athletes were in for a wild ride. The wind nearly knocked me flat many times, and all the while I held on with my good arm with everything I had. I rode my brakes down as much as I could. Headwind, then crosswind—the gusts moved back and forth and never eased up. My head was starting to drop once again, and for the first time in the race, after 165 miles, I started to worry. My good left arm wanted to give out on me, and I went right into prayer, asking the Lord to protect me and get me in safe.

With five miles to go, the tears started. I had given more than I knew I had. I had been on the bike for ten hours, and my good arm felt like it was about to fall off. "And, ladies and gentleman, coming in is Jason Lester!" Steve King's voice echoed through the trees and brought Day Two to a close. As I crossed the line, Doug, Annette, my buddy Rip, and others embraced me and sat me down. It was cold, and all I could think of was how badly I wanted soup and salt.

Now my focus was to get in the truck as fast as I could so we could get back to the house we had rented in the town of Waikaloa so Dawn could start my postrace massage. As we jumped in, I started drinking my postrace recovery formula: sixty grams of Carbo Pro and forty grams of protein to get me to the house, where I would start consuming gluten-free pasta by the boatload. Again, I was hurting. I felt like an engine that had been running on no oil for a thousand miles. Forty-five minutes later, Dawn lay me on her massage table and worked my torn, quivering muscles.

My goal was to be in bed by nine o'clock. I sat in bed

looking out at the ocean and realized this was all real. I think I got a total of four hours of sleep that night because my body was aching and I was tossing and turning. I had premade a 600-calorie carb drink in a bottle that I would reach for and sip each time I rolled over. So the night passed.

I was up again at 4 A.M., with the race start forty-five minutes away. I downed my 600 calories of carbs, and I ran in place in the bathroom just to see if my legs had any spring in them. Wow. I felt pretty good. The guns were locked and loaded. Suddenly I felt confident, and that brought a feeling of peace.

At the start, all the athletes gathered in a circle and joined hands. The race director, Jane Bockus, started our prerace ritual of blessing the race and the day. It was dark and cold with a few drops of rain, perfect running weather. I was worried about how much I might have left in the tank, but my mind was focused on the finish line. This was running, my forte. By the time Steve King started counting down the minutes, I was ready. When the gun went off, it was all about getting into a rhythm that was comfortable for me. But after five or six miles I got to thinking, *At what point do your legs give out?* And a voice inside me said, *Your body doesn't give out, Jason. Your mind doesn't give out. You keep going. You have enough nutrition. You've done the work. Nothing can stop you from accomplishing this challenge.*

I was in some kind of ultrazone. I must have spent the next eighteen miles noticing all the landmarks on the side of the Queen Ka'ahumanu Highway that I know so well, having trained on the Queen K almost daily for the past four years. Annette jumped in with me at about mile seven, and we started a long conversation about relationships. That's just what happens when you're trying to pass the time on a fifty-two-mile run.

I also found inspiration in my fellow competitors. At mile nineteen I got to talk with a couple of other athletes and learned about their running strategy for the day. I also talked with Warren, the athlete from the Big Island who I mentioned earlier. He ran the whole race with his heart rate at only 135 beats per minute (a more common heart rate for an Ultraman is around 145 or 150) and blew by me with one mile to go to the finish; I was so proud of him. Ten years earlier, Warren broke his back. The Ultraman World Championship was his comeback race to show the world that he was whole again. Talk about inspirational! Talking with other runners during the race reminds you that you're not alone out there and helps you realize that you're part of an incredible family just by being in the race.

The twenty-six-mile mark was about to pass, and it was *hot*. I was shoving ice down my pants and shirt and dumping bottles of ice water over my head. Doug had jumped in to pace me. I needed him: I was in pain from head to toe and had a throbbing headache on the right side of my skull. Doug hung with me in case my mind went blank, which it can do when you push yourself that far; competitors have run right off the course because their brains shift into neutral and they have no idea what they're doing.

I reached mile twenty-nine, then mile thirty-five. I said, "Doug, when we see the palm trees at the airport, we have seen Paradise Island." I was toast, but I would not turn from my purpose to be the first challenged athlete ever to finish this race. I kept asking Doug about landmarks on the side of the road, then I asked him to forgive me for asking over and over when the next hill was coming and how far we were from the airport.

The forty-mile mark came and went, and more and more locals started appearing and honking their horns. This gave me a boost of encouragement: I wasn't going to let Kona down. By mile forty-five, the only words I could say to Annette were "I think I may die." She replied in her calm, pure voice, "You look amazing, Jason. You're doing great, we are almost home." I was delusional. At that point I couldn't understand why anyone would want to do this— and then there I was. Kona International Airport. The palm trees. Paradise Island. I felt the Lord reaching down and saying, "I've got you, and I always have."

Even with the horns honking and people hanging out their windows yelling, the last ten kilometers felt like a hundred. My legs seemed to have weights attached to them, and my mind was out in left field with no glove. As we approached the energy lab I could briefly see over to the harbor, and from training on the Queen K daily I knew that right after the harbor, the old airport would be visible.

I will never forget those last eight miles. Friends started coming out to run with me, lending me their love and energy. Cars continued to drive by honking, people sticking their heads out the windows and yelling my name. People were cheering for me. I felt such humility because it was like I was representing my 'hood. I ran the next eight miles with tears of total exhaustion mixed with pure gratitude rolling down my face—gratitude for being allowed by God to do this.

As we approached Makala Road, it all made perfect sense—all the pain, agony, fear, and doubts. My questions were answered. As I made the turn and ran down toward the old airport, I began to speed up. Doug screamed, "You're only three minutes from breaking ten hours, let's pick it up!" If I'd had the strength, I would have laughed. I had been running on fumes for the last 10K, and Doug wanted me to pick it up? But I did. An extra burst of energy came from within me, and I could feel the Lord taking over. I began to sprint toward the finish line. Yes. There it was. The voice I had been waiting for. As I crossed the line Steve King screamed, "And, ladies and gentlemen, from right here in Kailua-Kona, Hawaii, let's give him a round of applause, Jason Lester!"

I finished in 10:01, barely missing my ten-hour goal. But it really didn't matter. I had done it. I had finished the Ultraman, the first challenged athlete to do it. Everyone who had helped me along the way gathered around me now, hugging me, congratulating me, and praising God.

• • •

Ultraman was a powerful experience for me. I had prayer warriors who had been asking God to help me find the strength and will to keep going. I knew they had my back. I knew my grandmother, who still has no idea what an Ironman or Ultraman is, believed in me and was my biggest fan. I knew that my tight circle of friends and supporters had my back as well. But I came to understand that in the end, there were really only two beings who had to believe in what I could accomplish: God and me.

Being a triathlete and being a Christian have something very important in common: they are both about faith. You study your faith, and you practice your faith, and you go out into the world, and you live as God would want you to live, by his example. In a triathlon you train, and then you go out and perform. You can't do either one without faith. If your faith in God isn't strong enough, doubt can shake it. And if your faith in your ability as a triathlete isn't strong enough, you're going to have a hard time doing what you must in order to compete or even enter races at all.

The King James Bible says that faith is "the substance of things hoped for, the evidence of things not seen." But it's also the ability to believe in things that haven't happened yet. Most of us don't believe a certain feat is possible until someone accomplishes it. Before the fact, it takes a leap of faith to believe that someone is capable of an act that defies common sense.

But as I said, outside of my tight circle of supporters, that faith was hard to find. When I was training for the Ultraman, people would say to me in amazement, "Do you realize you're going to swim 6.2 miles?" Like I hadn't thought about it up to that point. I know they didn't mean to discourage me, but I felt it anyway. I think people want to be supportive, but at the same time they live in a world where so many people promise so many things and don't deliver that they're afraid to believe in anybody. It's easier and safer to be skeptical and avoid having your heart broken. But when you're the person out there putting it all on the line, what you really hunger for is people who will take the risk of believing in you and say things like, "Jason, we're so excited you're doing this!" or "Dude, there's no doubt you're making it to the finish line!"

The hard truth is that we all want to be loved and have the approval and unqualified support of other people. But that's hard to come by in the best of times, and when you're doing something that others think is crazy, you're likely to find a lot more naysayers than supporters. That's when it's essential to remember **God's got your back.**

When the doubt and disbelief of the people around you drown out the encouragement and positive reinforcement, remember that God always believes in you. God's faith in you is infinitely more powerful than the faith of any one person, no matter how intense, because God will never put you in a situation without knowing that you have what it takes to succeed. That's not a guarantee that you *will* succeed, however; you've still got to perform and stick to your plan. But you wouldn't have the job or business opportunity or be standing in front of an audience as a speaker if you didn't have what it takes. As long as you're paying attention to where God is leading you, you'll always be where you're meant to be.

At the same time, if you're not ready to walk a certain path, you can do all the preparation you like and things may still not fall into place. If you've been trying for years to start a business or run a race and doors just won't open for you, there might be a reason. You're probably trying to force something to happen before God thinks you're ready. You have some learning and growing to do first. When the time comes, he will open the door and the things you've been trying to make happen will start coming to pass. In short, where you are right now is right where you're supposed to be. When your mind and spirit are ready to take you down a new path, God will open a new door for you.

I've stopped looking for acceptance of what I do. I don't need it from outside myself. Does that sound lonely? Well, it is, a little. This can be a very lonely sport. You train hour after hour by yourself. You don't have anybody to answer to. No one but your coach and a few friends cares whether you get to the starting line or the finish line. I can't tell you how many days and nights I have questioned what I'm doing and why I'm doing it, and then God speaks up and reminds me that this is my purpose in life.

At the end of the day, I know that God's got my back through all my decisions. To him, there are no good and bad choices. There are just decisions that take you farther from him and decisions that bring you closer. God allows you to go down the paths that lead you away from him—drugs, divorce, debt—so you will learn and become wiser. God is going to have your back after good decisions and also after the ones that were not so wise. He is never going to leave your side.

God will ensure that some other people have your back, too. Their love and positive attitude are a big help when you're sticking your neck out. But remember, even though you will almost certainly find a few core folks who believe in you no matter what, you'll likely find more doubters. When you're pushing the envelope, that's what happens. But all it takes is one person to have total faith in you.

For me, that's Dave. As a world-class triathlete and a top-five finisher in the Masters division, he knows what it takes physically, mentally, and spiritually to do what I want to do. He knows that just as it takes only one person to believe, it also takes only one person to poison you with negative thinking. That's why his feedback is always positive, his advice always constructive, and his plans always outrageous. He knows I love to be pushed and dared to do what I haven't done before.

In the end, we all need a balance: a small core of people who support us unconditionally, and a connection with God's infinite faith, which helps us endure all the messages about what we can't accomplish. Both are crucial; you need a supportive environment to succeed in this sport.

Today, even with all the things I have accomplished, I often still assume that people will doubt me. Some do, but it doesn't bother me anymore. I have my core of supporters who will always have faith in me, and that's enough. The best I can hope for is that when I cross the next finish line, somebody in the doubter camp will find their jaw hitting the ground as they think, *Wow, I was wrong about that guy.*

I hope the person's next thought is *Hey, I wonder what I could do if I really put my mind to it and gave it all I had?* That's why I do this, to remind people that when God's got your back, you're capable of great things.

7

JUST SAY YES

"Don't be afraid to go out on a limb. That's where the fruit is."
—**Will Rogers**

It was another killer swim, this time at Ultraman Canada in August 2008. I was three miles into my six miles and trying, like I always do, to put the distance out of my mind and concentrate on getting from point A to point B. The whole time my assistance kayaker, Derrie, had been feeding me positive words and thoughts: "You're doing great, Jason!" "You look fantastic, Jason!" Every so often I would spare a look up at the kayak and see her smile. I eat that stuff up. Encouragement is like rocket fuel. I felt myself getting stronger as I fed off her energy.

Then, at the four-and-a-half-mile mark, the thing I had always dreaded happened. I know that swimming these brutal distances puts a terrible strain on my good left arm, and I've always had the fear in the back of my mind that one day I might shred my rotator cuff, pop a tendon, or tear my deltoid muscle. So far it hadn't happened. But suddenly I started feeling a sharp, stabbing pain in my shoulder. My stomach dropped. I knew I had to stop and rest and try to figure out what was going on, so I swam over and told Derrie what I was feeling. Bless her, she kept her cool and knew exactly what to do. She gave me some Advil to take the edge off the pain and massaged my shoulder while I treaded water next to her kayak. But I knew I had to do another mile and a half and finish before the six-hour cutoff time, so I soon started stroking and kicking again. I didn't know what was going on in my shoulder, but I hoped it was nothing more serious than a muscle strain.

I swam for a half mile more when *pop!* went my shoulder at mile five. Instantly I was unable to pull my arm back toward my body; my shoulder simply would not rotate in its capsule. I had either ruptured the tendon in my shoulder or had such a bad case of tendonitis that my shoulder simply shut down. Either way, I was stuck. I couldn't do my normal swim stroke. I could reach my arm out, but when I tried to pinwheel my arm back underwater to propel myself along and ready for the next stroke—nothing. I willed my arm to move. Nothing. My Ultraman was over. "God, no!" I shouted. I was not going to let it end like this. I started dog-paddling for twenty minutes so I could keep moving. How was I possibly going to stay in the race? My time had been good up until now, but I would slow to a crawl if I tried to dog-paddle the remaining mile-plus. I would almost certainly miss the cutoff, and my day would be over.

Then, I don't know if it was God or the Advil kicking in,

but the pain started to fall away. It didn't disappear, but it was manageable. I could work with that kind of pain, so I started paddling again. Then I saw the buoy that indicates the turn toward the finish. It always reminds me of when square-rig sailors used to see Cape Horn as they rounded the tip of South America; passing that marker meant better things were ahead. Adrenaline shot through my body. I knew if I sucked it up and found a way, I could finish the hardest swim of my brief triathlon career. So I improvised a new stroke, keeping my arm straight and pulling it down and across my body like a gunfighter pulling his pistol from the holster on the opposite hip. Since my shoulder didn't have to rotate, the tendon I had injured didn't come into play; I was doing all the work with my deltoid and pectoral muscles. It definitely wasn't pretty, but it got me moving at a decent speed and, most important, without searing pain. I started kicking like crazy and pulled for shore.

When I heard the people screaming on the sand and I knew I was home free. Like I said, I ride those currents of love and support the way a hovercraft rides on air. I heard the announcer saying my name, and that gave me the last push I needed. I got to the finish under the cutoff time and was surrounded by friends and supporters congratulating me, but I immediately saw what I had accomplished. Some tourists were staring at me from their seats, mouths open, dumbfounded. They hadn't realized that I had the use of only one arm, and now it was dawning on them. I love surprising people with what I can do because then maybe they'll think differently about their own limitations.

Even though I still had a double marathon ahead of me,

I had taken on the biggest challenge of my career as a triathlete and managed, somehow, to survive. You see, I wasn't even supposed to be in the water in the first place.

• • •

I had intended to use the run portion of Ultraman Canada as a warm-up for the 2008 Ultraman World Championship. I had plenty of experience running, but I had never run fifty-two miles. In the Ultraman there is a relay division in which several teams compete, each with a different athlete doing the swim, cycle, and run. I asked the race director to put me together with a local cyclist and swimmer; I would handle the run portion of the race so I could test my body in the double marathon.

Then, about four weeks before the race, the director contacted me to let me know that our swimmer had dropped out and that we needed to find a replacement. It took me about five minutes after reading that e-mail to make the decision that I would swim 6.2 miles. Fear never entered my mind. But was I nervous? You bet. Fear and nerves are different. Fear is the suspicion that you may not have what it takes to triumph when faced with a challenge, which could be anything from finishing a marathon to asking someone out on a date. Nerves come when you're champing at the bit to start something but you're forced to wait. That energy has to go somewhere, so it comes out as prerace jitters or backstage shakes. I didn't doubt my ability to handle the swim. But I was amped up about it, and I knew I wouldn't relax until I was actually in the water.

As usual, God had different plans than I did. I wanted to ease into the Ultraman distances, testing out the run portion first. But he wanted me to jump into my weakest area as well. I had forgotten that God doesn't always let us wait until the stars align to ask us to try something. Sometimes he just opens the door and says, "Go!" This swim would be well outside my comfort zone, but so what? Doing a triathlon is outside any person's comfort zone, but thousands of people do it anyway. The choice was simple: I could let my anxiety stop me from taking a risk that carried a potentially big upside, or I could let my faith become stronger.

I replied to the e-mail and said that I would do the swim. Then I contacted Dave and told him what I had in mind. God love him, he just blinked and said, "We have work to do." Then we got down to business. With Dave, it's always about a game plan. He comes up with the plan, and I execute it.

Four weeks later I made my way to the starting area at Ultraman Canada and met my support crew for the first time. That's common unless you live near the race; the directors find local athletes who are willing to help out, but we don't know who they are until race day. I met my crew, and everything was fine until we headed for the starting line and put the kayak in the water. I was putting on my wet suit, and I asked Derrie for some duct tape.

"What for?" she asked.

"So I can tape my right arm to my body," I said.

She looked at me like I'd said I was going to use the tape to build a boat and sail the 6.2 miles. Then it hit her that I didn't have the use of my arm. She gave me a look that said at the same time, "You're nuts," and, "Can you really do this?" In her shoes I would have done the same thing. But then she handed me the tape and smiled. I think she dug my audacity and the spirit of what I was going to try to do. I did manage to finish the swim and, two days later, finish the run. I was a little the worse for wear, but I still made it, and that's the important thing.

That day I learned so much about myself as a distance athlete that I hardly know where to begin. I learned that I needed to train my left arm and shoulder even more intensely so they would stand the strain of doing all the work in the swim. I learned that I had the endurance to get through an Ultraman-length swim under the cutoff time, a massive boost for my confidence. I learned that while the sight of me competing was going to shock some people, there were those who loved the fact that I was out there trying and would back me all the way. Most important, I learned once again that God was right. He laid out a path for me that led me out of my comfort zone, and it proved to be a great blessing for me. That day in Canada led directly to my racing in and finishing the Ultraman World Championship just a few months later.

But if I hadn't said yes to the opportunity God brought my way, I might not have learned any of it. Without more intense left arm training, I might have popped my shoulder tendon at Ultraman Hawaii, the race I had bet all my chips on. Maybe I would have found out during that swim that I didn't have the endurance to complete such a long swim. Perhaps the only thing that would have happened was that I would have wondered every day, "Could I have done it?" If I hadn't said yes, I would have been saying no to something that God was working to guide me toward, and I've long since learned that when God is holding a door open, you walk through. You don't ask questions or worry. You just walk through and see what's on the other side. In other words, **just say yes**.

As you go through life, God is going to present you with opportunities to leave your comfort zone and stretch yourself. When he does, you're going to be nervous, to say the least. You might be scared witless. You might find a dozen ways to rationalize not taking the risk in front of you. Do it anyway. Recognize that when you have those feelings, God is holding out a hand and saying, "I'm going to guide you over this bridge to new territory, and if you look down and see the long drop you're going to be terrified, but if you trust me and keep walking I'll reveal wonders to you."

Not long after the accident that cost me the use of my arm, I discovered the importance of saying yes. What choice did I have? I was damaged goods as an athlete, so if I accepted the judgment of people who assumed I couldn't play baseball or football anymore, I would end up sitting in my room, watching other guys play, gaining weight, and being miserable. Risking my neck playing sports with one arm seemed like the better choice, and it was. As soon as my pals helped me dive back into high school sports, I felt alive. Sure, there were uncomfortable moments. I had to learn to do many familiar motions all over again, from catching and throwing a baseball to lacing up my football cleats. Sometimes it was embarrassing; other times it was scary. But I was never tempted to quit.

Being a triathlete is the same way. This sport makes unbelievable demands on the human body, and there's no way to know while you're training how you're going to perform in the middle of a race. Let me tell you, training is *not* competition. During a race you have to deal with nerves and adrenaline, you have other competitors trying to bury you, and you have weather conditions you can't predict. It's not a comfort-zone kind of experience, but that's why a lot of us do it. If you ask one hundred triathletes why they compete, ninety-nine of them are going to say it's for the challenge; they want to see how far they can push themselves.

That's how we're wired—not just me and other distance racers, but you, too. Human beings are designed to push limits and take risks and discover new frontiers that a few years ago would have been called insane. But many people choose a comfortable life instead, with the things that bring them that comfort—the house, the job, the car—becoming more important than pushing their own boundaries and getting closer to God. When the window dressing of your life means more to you than your personal evolution, you stop growing. You settle. You forget how thrilling it is to be out there on the high wire trying something you're not comfortable with, whether it's moving to a new city where you don't know anybody or going back to college when you're twice the age of the average freshman. Sure, it's frightening too, but that's how you know you're alive.

When I say yes to a race and I'm in the middle of the course, it hurts. It's a struggle. It's painful and exhausting. But it's nothing I haven't met before, and the joy I experience is so much greater than the discomfort. Each time I race, I'm stepping out of my comfort zone and into a place where anything can happen. Sure, I could injure myself. I could crash on my bike. I could get my butt kicked by another competitor. But I could also find new reserves of strength or learn something new about myself that will improve my performance in future races. The point is if you don't say yes, how will you know what you're not experiencing?

For me, a race is more than an athletic event. It's healing time. I may be running or biking in a triathlon and feeling great, but for miles I'll have tears streaming down my face. A race gives me mourning time alone with my thoughts and with God. I never really mourned my father's death; I cried at his funeral only because everyone else did. I didn't really grasp the significance of the accident that wrecked my arm, so I never mourned that loss either. People who see me probably assume I'm crying because I'm hurting, but I'm not. It's a spiritual and mental healing time for me. It's my time to try and place a few more pieces in the puzzle that is my life, to add a few more brushstrokes to the painting.

If I had said no to athletics after my injury or to competing in triathlons after seeing the Ironman in 2004, I might never have had the chance to experience that kind of healing and ecstasy. I might well have followed my father into an early grave, too. My family has a history of heart disease, and I grew up heavy until I discovered distance running. I've busted my tail for years to get my body into the kind of shape it's in; it didn't happen overnight, over a year, or even over five years. To be exact, I started running and hiking Camelback Mountain in Phoenix when I was fifteen, and I became addicted to it. Soon I started timing myself. I once rode my bike fifteen miles to Squaw Peak, put the bike on my back, hiked to the top, then came down and rode home.

I even had to overcome an eating disorder that I developed in my twenties because I was worried about gaining too much weight to compete in races. I had terrible eating habits as a kid, then became a vegetarian at thirteen, so I was always preoccupied with food. In my mind, if I stayed slim, I was in race shape. It's taken me twenty years to get as fit and healthy as I am today.

When something beckons you into unknown territory, do you find yourself automatically saying no? We all do it. My first impulse upon reading the e-mail from the race director about doing the Ultraman swim was to reply, "No, thanks"—until I realized that it was God's handiwork. The secret is recognizing what a potential risk can be: an invitation from God to discover something new about yourself. It's God offering you a chance to grow in wisdom, strength, perception, or faith. Start training yourself to see risks and scary situations as communiqués from the Lord, not just as things to avoid, and you'll find your view of life changing.

I experienced one of these situations during a race in Boise, Idaho, with my fellow teammates. We were cycling and all of a sudden rain began crashing down on our heads. It was a falling wall of water like ball bearings fired from cannons. With it came sheets of lightning and blasts of thunder that made our inner ears rumble. It was primal. I couldn't take off my sunglasses, which were so fogged up that I could barely see, because the water was falling so hard that it would instantly blind me. Racers were ducking for cover, but I kept going. It was a challenge to see who would maintain their faith that they could come through. I felt the fear and welcomed it because I knew that God was urging me to push through it and find something greater on the other side. When the sun came back out later in that race, I found it.

• • •

When you say yes to the opportunities that frighten or intimidate you, God will always do two things. He will give you gifts, and he will humble you. Most of the time the gift and the humility go hand in hand. The true gift that he's given me is my will to never quit. I'm not faster or stronger or a better swimmer than many of the other guys on the course. The thing God gave me when I followed his lead into distance running was the will to endure the pain and tedium and exhaustion—and even learn to love it. My gift is the ability to make myself keep going and do what I need to do when my body wants to throw in the towel.

God will also take you out of your comfort zone to teach you humility. This is crucial because success brings such an incredible high that it is easy to become arrogant about it. God won't allow arrogance because it will ruin everything he has in mind for you. Pride breeds complacency and laziness and contempt for the people who helped you get where you are. It has brought many, many professional athletes down.

When I first came out to Los Angeles after leaving Arizona State, I took an internship at a sports marketing firm. Before long I was director of marketing, which involved working with professional boxers and sitting ringside for big pay-per-view boxing events. I'll never forget attending the premier of the movie *Hurricane* and sitting next to Denzel

Washington. I was thinking to myself, *I have made it*. But even though it sounds like I had hit the jackpot, I had really turned aside from the path God had in mind. God had bigger and better plans for me. My flesh fought with my spirit month after month because I didn't want to let this lifestyle go. I had become proud of what I had done, even though I hadn't made any of it happen myself.

So God humbled me. Whether it was the drugs, the eating disorder, broken relationships, or bad finances, it was all his way of reminding me in stark terms who I was and what I was destined for. I got out of that business because God let me know that I didn't belong there.

God humbles us even as he gives us gifts because he doesn't want us to take our gifts or our vision of the future for granted. When I won the ESPY Award for Best Male Athlete with a Disability in 2009, it was an incredible experience, an acknowledgment of all the risks I had taken and all the times I had said yes to the visions God put before me without understanding the reasons why. Right after I won I did dozens of interviews, talked with new sponsors, and rode the roller-coaster of fame a little bit. I was even an honored guest at an Arizona Diamondbacks game. It was pretty seductive.

While I was in Phoenix my attorney threw me a party. Going home for this event reminded me of my roots. I had the chance to speak in front of my high school varsity football team on the same field that I once played on. At the party, fifty or so friends, family, teachers, and coaches came to support me and congratulate me. I stood up in front of them all, microphone in hand, and I was at a loss for words.

I put my head down and thanked God not only for humbling me, but also for giving me the inspiration to continue to follow my passion of being an athlete.

When I could finally speak, I looked out into the crowd. For the first time in thirty-five years, I got to thank my eighty-two-year-old grandmother, my number one fan. She's never watched me race, but she's never doubted me. What she does best is pray for me. I couldn't have gotten where I am without her. I was able to thank my high school coaches, grade school friends, and my family for never allowing me to give up. I couldn't have gotten where I am without them either. I'm humbled to have a team behind me. I always say that God is my owner, coach Dave is the quarterback, my family and friends and fans are my offensive line, and I'm simply running the ball.

The people at my high school were not the ones who knew me as an Ultraman and ESPY winner. They knew me simply as Jason, the pudgy kid from down the street or the dude they once played baseball with. Your roots are who you are, and you're nothing without them. I have a core of close buddies who really love me, and I would be nothing without them. Even though I've been on a high for the last three years, seeing all those people reminded me why I am the luckiest guy on the planet.

I'm still just me. I've accomplished a lot and won some awards, but I'm nothing without God. Yes, I've structured my life to allow these things to happen, and I'm receiving praise for the hard work I've put in, but I'm no different as a man. The only thing I've learned to do is to welcome those times when God gives me the chance to try what scares me.

The more uncomfortable something makes me, the faster I rush through the door to give it a shot. I know there's going to be a gift on the other side. If you're prepared to be humble and open-minded, there are doors opening for you, too. If you hear God calling you, *just say yes*.

8

NEVER STOP

"He that endureth to the end shall be saved."
—Matthew 10:22

I had never raced in heat like this. I'm not sure that British Columbia had ever *seen* heat like this. I got on my bike with ninety miles of climbing in front of me, and the first thought that flashed through my brain was *My God, it's hot.* That tells you something: Mr. Never Think Negatively was thinking about how brutal the day was going to be. That wasn't like me, but then, this was heat like I'd never experienced.

I got thirty or forty miles into the first cycling stage, near Okanagan Falls over the Richter Pass, a route with just under 4,100 feet of climb, when I felt the oven turn on with full force. Even on the best of days, that much elevation gain will rip your guts out no matter how fit you are, but I and the rest of the competitors were tackling it in the midst of one of the gnarliest heat waves ever to hit British Columbia. It had to be more than 110 degrees in the canyons, so hot I felt like I couldn't breathe.

In race situations like that, you have basically one lifeline: ice. Lots of ice. There are no support bikes allowed on the Ultraman course, so my crew would catch up to me in their support van when I'd slow down and stuff plastic bags filled with ice down the back of my jersey. When I stopped for a break, they were putting ice rags on my neck. I was downing melted ice water by the gallon just to keep from dehydrating and getting heatstroke. I was swimming in ice, bathing in it. My team went through six ten-pound bags of ice on that first day just dumping it on my head, putting ice cubes in my mouth, and pouring freezing water onto my helmet to keep my head cool. It was a constant struggle to keep my body from dangerously overheating.

Competing in blistering heat is probably the hardest thing an extreme distance racer can do. Even in normal conditions, the body begins to heat up as you cycle or run farther and farther. This isn't a problem in the swim stage because the water conducts the heat away from your skin. But once you start cycling or running, the body has to work harder and harder to keep itself cool. You start to sweat, which cools the body through evaporation. Meanwhile, the hypothalamus, the part of the brain that controls thermoregulation, signals the blood vessels to send more blood to the surface of the skin, where it can release heat. This works fine until you're hammering away at a bike almost straight uphill.

When you're putting your body through the intense demands of exercise, blood also needs to flow to the muscles to satisfy their screams for oxygen. So now you've got two competing demands: the skin wants circulation to cool your body, and your muscles want it to keep you moving. If your skin can't get what it needs, you'll start to boil over and head toward heat exhaustion. If your muscles can't get what they need, you'll slow down, cramp, and stop altogether. It's a nasty tug-of-war.

I honestly didn't know how I was going to make it to the end of Day One. I still had five more hours of torture in front of me—thousands of feet of climb yet to come—all through a blast furnace. And I'd already swum six miles. I started to wonder when I would blow up. When would I say, "Enough," and just set my bike down? I had seen a few other competitors do it, overcome by the heat.

Then I looked around, and my support van was gone. My team had stayed close to help me stay cool, but now they were nowhere to be found. I started to panic because my fluid bottles were empty. I rode for a good thirty minutes with no liquids and no carbohydrate drinks, thinking that my team must have had to stop to get more ice. I could see another competitor up ahead of me, and I knew I could ask his crew for an extra bottle of water. When my crew finally showed up, I yelled, "You can't leave me like that or I'll die."

I wasn't being melodramatic. At that level of exertion in that kind of blistering heat, heatstroke is a real danger. Your body loses the ability to cool itself, you stop sweating, your internal temperature can rise as high as 106 or more, and your organs start to shut down. People die from heatstroke. I was in for the toughest challenge of my racing career.

• • •

It was Ultraman Canada 2009, and it was my chance to do something that only fourteen other people have ever done: complete both the Ultraman World Championship in Hawaii and Ultraman Canada in the same calendar year. Preparing for and enduring just one of these races pushes most extreme athletes to their absolute limit, but as more than one person has told me, I'm a bit of a psycho.

But things were turning out to be complicated. The wicked heat wave blanketing the Pacific Northwest had given Seattle its highest-ever temperature just a few days before, and going into the race everyone knew that the heat, not the other athletes, was going to be the real opponent. Still, I was confident that with my team helping me and God at my back, I would reach my goal.

It was already hot on the morning of Day One, but the waters of Skaha Lake—about a four-hour drive from Vancouver in the heart of the British Columbia backcountry— were about 75 and perfect for the six-mile swim. It was a gorgeous, calm morning, and I could see all the way across the lake to the finish. Going to the starting line, I was confident, and when I got in the water I felt even better. I got off to a strong start and was having a terrific swim.

Then at about the halfway point, something happened. It's hard to describe: I felt a current going with me, carrying me, and I started swimming faster and faster. It was a nearly effortless gain in speed. I looked around, and none of the other swimmers seemed to be riding the current; it was just me. It was one of the most amazing experiences I've ever had in a race. My kayaker shouted, "Are you sure you're going to be able to maintain this pace, Jason?" I just grinned and kept swimming. I wasn't sure of anything at that point, but I felt like a dolphin. Nothing hurt, I didn't feel out of breath, and I was swimming faster than I had ever swum before.

I thought back to the Ultraman in Hawaii, when I had shot right into the heart of a jellyfish colony, and the panic that their stings had brought on. This was the complete opposite feeling. It was pure joy, pure freedom. *What are you up to, God?* I thought. Clearly, he was behind this sudden surge of power that was carrying me along. I wasn't sure why he was giving me such a gift at this stage in the race, when I was still fresh with so much grueling work still to go, but when God blesses you, you don't question. You send out your silent thanks and praise and keep pushing. That's what I did.

I reached the finish of the swim and pulled myself from the lake at 4:43:17—the third slowest time among all the swimmers, but I've never worried about that. I would be getting into my strengths now, the cycling and running stages. I jumped on my bike—and immediately slammed into the wall of heat. As I headed for Route 97, which would carry me south toward Richter Pass and close to the Canadian border, I realized why God had given me that beautiful push of effortless energy in the swim: he knew that the day's cycling would be sheer hell.

● ● ●

As Day One progressed and my body grew hotter and hotter, I felt blessed and honored that Gary Wang, eleven-time finisher of the Western States 100 (one of the country's major ultramarathons) and a nine-time Ultraman finisher, was on my crew. Gary knew about all situations and all conditions. I didn't need to tell him much because he could see from my face that I was hurting. When my crew returned, I told them, "I need a bottle of water with my carbs in it, and I need a bottle of ice water to throw on my body." They immediately handed me both bottles. In a triathlon you're supposed to drink a minimum of twenty-four ounces of water an hour, but with the heat and the way I was perspiring, those limits went out the window. I needed electrolytes and carbohydrates just to keep my muscles working. I downed the water and doused myself and immediately felt better.

Then at about mile sixty, I started passing people. I'm usually one of the later athletes out of the water, and because the bike stage is one of my strengths I usually pass a few guys to get to the middle of the pack. But I was passing them on hills now. As I watched the other competitors, I saw that they too were roasting and on the verge of heat exhaustion. We were all struggling to keep body and will together and make it to mile ninety. The question wasn't, "Who's the most fit?" or "Who has the use of what arm?" but "Who is going to surrender to the heat?"

I knew that it wouldn't be me. I knew that God had helped me save energy in the swim so I could endure this ride. Not long before, I had been sure I was going to bonk.

But I decided I would rather give it everything I had and bonk than hold back. I didn't want to disappoint my coach, my team, or the foundation that I mentioned earlier. It's called the Never Stop Foundation for a reason. I said to myself, *Dude, you live in Hawaii. You're used to the heat. Suck it up.* I felt my will toughen. I knew I was going to make it.

I passed a few more guys and finished the day in eighteenth place. There was no celebrating, though; two more days in the oven were still to come. The race director drove home the point when he told us that we had to prepare for Day Two because it was going to be *really* hot. When you hear that, the first thing you do is trip out a little. The second thing you do is start preparing mentally. I would have to ride 170 miles—almost twice as far as I had ridden on Day One—in the same kind of heat or worse while climbing a total of 5,774 feet. Anticipating that kind of struggle can mess with your head. So I focused on preparation: rest, fluids, and strategies to stay cool, stay alive, and keep going.

Day Two dawned just as scorching as Day One. It was like riding inside a blast furnace. The heat washed everything else out of my mind; it was like a liquid pouring from the sky, searing the lungs of every competitor. All I could think about was continuing to pedal and trying to stay cool. As we rode from Penticton past Okanagan Lake, the temperature increased. I knew that if it continued, athletes were going to struggle by the time we got to a portion of the route affectionately nicknamed The Wall. I was determined I would not be one of them, but I wasn't as confident as I have been in the past that I could endure this. The main goals on

Day Two are to not overexert yourself and to consume as many calories as you can, with your eye on Day Three's long run. My goal became staying upright.

Then suddenly God turned on the cosmic air conditioner. Gradually, the column of cyclists rode into a pocket of cooler air, and you could hear a collective sigh of relief echo down the road. The temperature dropped into the eighties, but it felt like the Arctic. I said a silent prayer of thanks and really started pumping. By the time I rolled into Princeton Arena, where massage therapists were waiting to work on sore athletes, I had gained two more spots for sixteenth place.

Day Three was effortless after what I had already endured. The weather was gorgeous, and I seemed to have bottomless energy. I ran the first marathon (26.2 miles) in 4:45 and the second one in 4:48, times I was happy with after racing 230 miles in the water and on a bike the previous two days. On the back of the support vehicle was a huge Never Stop Foundation banner; I remember looking at it for the nine-plus hours I was on the running course. It was a reminder to me: *You're not going to let down this foundation and the people who support you.* And I didn't. I crossed the finish of Ultraman Canada in fourteenth place overall out of twenty-seven athletes, praising God at every step.

• • •

God created us to be limitless, but we set limits on what we think we can do. We base our expectations on what others tell us and on our fears of what we can't achieve. Our inner voice can be like a terrorist whispering to us: "You're not strong enough. You're not smart enough. You're not good enough." Those whispers were what I heard during the first day of cycling at Ultraman Canada. We've all heard them. They encourage us to find an excuse to give up. They tell us it's okay to quit *this time*. What they don't tell us is that each time we give in, each time we stop before we achieve our goal, it becomes a little easier to quit the next time.

The lesson that I discovered that day in the Canadian heat was that if we listen to God's voice rather than our negative inner voice, we can transcend our supposed limits. In God's words: **Never stop.**

Ever since I was six years old training on the baseball fields of Phoenix with my father, I've lived those words. In my athletic life, quitting was never an option. Being tired wasn't a reason. Being bored wasn't a reason. Being sore? Definitely not a reason. I took batting practice until I had blisters the size of nickels on my hands, then came back for more the next day.

In fact, I think my relentlessness began even sooner than that. When I was young, I was in day care and my father came to pick me up. When he arrived at the center, the teacher pointed him toward the backyard playground. I had been running around the perimeter of the yard, she said, for about four hours. Dad told me about the episode years later, but I remember how it felt. Running gave me a sense of consistency and freedom; I could turn my mind off and take pleasure in the simple predictability of left foot, right foot, left foot, right foot. I don't remember ever getting tired.

"Never stop" means that when you set aside your fears and doubts and realize who God made you to be, you find the endurance and persistence to soldier on until you achieve any goal. It means keeping your eyes on the road—left foot, right foot—and knowing that if you are doing the right things, then over time blessings will come to you. No matter what you go through, you keep pushing forward.

We're results-oriented people. We don't care about the process; we just want the product. Instead of working out and eating healthy food and losing weight gradually to enhance health and quality of life, millions of people take diet pills and have liposuction to lose pounds. They simply don't have the patience. They don't understand that who you become as you progress toward your goal is the real reward.

Training for a triathlon is not just a physical journey. It's a transformative experience. To get ready for a race, I punish myself seven days a week—training for twenty to twenty-five hours a week, swimming lap after lap in the pool, working out at the gym, eating like a monk. If I was focused only on the goal—getting to the race—I would probably never complete my training. The process would just be too slow. I think many other distance athletes would say the same thing.

But a triathlon is not about the destination, at least not entirely. It's also about the joy of the journey. So every step, every mile, changes who I am. By the time I get to the starting line of an Ultraman, I'm more than a fit body. I'm also an iron will that's incapable of stopping. I'm a centered mind capable of meditating with God at every step. I'm different than when I started. Knowing there's a purpose to all of it makes it easier to push myself through pain, blood, and exhaustion.

There's a reason that my foundation is called Never

Stop—it's the motto of my life. Training for a triathlon is like training for life—you have to structure and prioritize and deal with setbacks and roadblocks on the way to the finish line. The only way you get to that finish is to keep going. Life doesn't give you the option of pressing the pause button and quitting. If you do quit, giving up on your dream, you become a zombie, shuffling through life, feeling nothing. Sadly, lots of people live like that, but that's not living; it's existing without the joy and purpose that life can bring. The only way you get anything worthwhile in this life is to never, ever give up. You have much more strength than you know.

God has given me the will to focus not on my disability but on my *ability*. Instead of looking for an excuse to stop, I find the miracle in the experience while it's happening: the amazing current in the lake that buoyed me forward, the reserves of energy I find when I think I have none left, and the beauty and purity of the time I have with God when everything else is just stripped away and it's just me, the road, and him.

• • •

What could you have achieved in your life if you hadn't stopped in the past? Where would you be if you'd kept going when things started to get boring or frustrating or the results didn't come as quickly as you would have liked? Most people stop far short of their goals because, well, because reaching goals is hard. Change is hard. If it were easy, everyone would do it.

But what if you didn't give yourself the option to quit? What if, instead of worrying about some short-term goal, you just savored the fact that you were doing what was right for your body, your relationships, your career, or your spiritual life? If you could see doing the right thing for yourself as its own reward, you would take pleasure in every difficult step. You wouldn't worry about getting to the finish line because the race—the transformation of body, mind, and spirit—would be the prize. When you think that way, it becomes more difficult to allow yourself to quit. Eventually you start craving experiences that stretch and challenge you, and you view each one as another opportunity to prove to yourself that you've evolved.

My own fitness journey is a perfect example of what I mean. At age thirteen I weighed about 140 pounds, what I weigh now. But the weight was mostly fat, not lean muscle. As a kid, I was always looked at as husky, and, growing up, I was often teased. I was also afraid that I would suffer a heart attack like my father. By the time I reached junior high, I was seriously motivated to change things. I changed my diet and I started exercising more. It wasn't something that I was taught or that I read about; it just happened. I trained; it didn't matter if it was 40 degrees out in the Arizona winter or 115 in the summer.

Thirty-ninth Avenue in Phoenix became my first Laboratory. I remember seeing my friends riding their bikes and skateboarding past me as I ran. I remember seeing a video of Mike Tyson when he was fifteen years old, training for countless hours. I then realized what it was going to take for me to become a champion. I started running and cycling ridiculous distances with a manic intensity. The weight came off. Today I have blood pressure and cholesterol readings so low that my doctor can barely measure them, but that didn't come about overnight. I had a vision, given to me by God, of who I could be. I knew with every step, with every healthy meal that I ate, I was moving closer to realizing that vision. I didn't let myself get discouraged. I never stopped.

Building muscles is like training for your first triathlon: you can't obsess over the day-to-day results or you'll quit. If you're lifting weights, from one day to the next you're not going to see much of a change in the mirror. If you're training for the swim and you start out able to do only one hundred yards in the pool, you might feel bummed when you can still do only a hundred by the end of the first week of workouts. That's when you have to trust the limitless potential that God placed within you and keep your eyes on the big picture.

Do what's right, consistent, and disciplined. Pushing yourself is essential to building six-pack abs, competing in a triathlon, or succeeding at just about any goal in life. You go through the motions every day and take pleasure in knowing that you're changing yourself each time you do. Think about that: every time you roll out of bed at 5:00 A.M. to run ten miles, every time you sock away another five hundred dollars in your 401(k) instead of spending it, every day you say no to lighting up another cigarette, you're becoming someone stronger, more disciplined, and closer to God. That's all the reward anyone needs in the short term. In the long term, all those days that you answered the bell eventually add up to what you've been dreaming of. For me it was doing Ironman and Ultraman. For you, it might be your own distance race or something entirely different. Either way, getting to your finish line is sweet.

In the Old Testament book of Exodus, Moses leads the Hebrews out of bondage and into the desert in search of the Promised Land. But they don't reach the land of milk and honey overnight. They wander in the desert for forty years— a year for each day they had spies in the land of Canaan, says the book of Numbers. It is only through supreme faith that they finally come to the land that was promised to them by God. If they had given up and chosen to make do in the desert because waiting for God to lead them out had become too frustrating, Israel might not exist today. Perseverance is *everything*.

These days, "never stop" continues to be my mantra. It sustains me through Ironman and Ultraman races, and it will sustain me through the next level of extreme events that I or someone else is dreaming up. Because my goal is to be doing this at seventy years old. I want to be at the starting line with all the thirty- and forty-year-old guys and gals. Maybe they'll stare and maybe they'll wonder, but I'll smile, knowing that my knowledge and the lessons I've learned throughout my life allow me to remain competitive. My wisdom will make up for my age, and when the swim stage starts, I'll amaze the young rebels, inspiring them to pull and kick and pedal and run harder and faster than they ever have before, just to keep up with a senior citizen.

That's the dream God has put in my heart. It won't be possible unless I never stop.

9

GET BEYOND YOURSELF

"The purpose of life is a life of purpose."
—**Robert Byrne, author**

The most incredible blessing of the 2008 Ironman World Championship was not that I finished the race or that I performed well. That was fantastic, but this was better: *I was actually able to use my right arm in the race.*

Most people think of my paralyzed right arm as being a handicap only in the swim stage of a triathlon. That's understandable. Having only one arm means that I have to get extra power from my legs, and when I get out of the water my legs are already burning. The other racers have hardly used their legs at all. Plus, swimming with one arm means my entire race rests on my left shoulder and elbow. One torn rotator cuff or popped ligament, and I'm a spectator.

But my paralyzed wing is also a big problem in the cycling stage. I have to drink water and carbohydrate drinks throughout the cycling stage so that I can keep going for 112 miles. That's no problem for someone who has two good arms: you just hold onto the handlebars with one arm while you grab your water bottle with the other and take a drink. When your bottle is empty, you reach down onto your bike frame with one arm and snatch a fresh bottle from its rack. But for me, it was never that simple. I couldn't hold the handlebars with my right arm.

One of the things that fans and even family don't understand about having a physical challenge is that it's very taxing on the mind. I have to think ten steps ahead in everything I do. If I'm carrying something down the street, I have to figure out how I'm going to open the door. I'm constantly alert to my surroundings, and in a race one of the things I'm alert to is that I have to stop to drink water. It's exasperating because once I'm in a zone on the bike, I don't want to stop, but I know that if I don't get enough fluids and calories into my body during the ride I will cramp up. It can feel like a no-win situation.

I adapted to the need to drink during a race by using a bottle rack that put the bottle right in front of me, where I could lean down and drink through a straw. But when it came time to refill a container, I was hosed. I had no choice but to stop my bike and use my left arm to refill my bottle. Since I might be doing twenty miles per hour or more on the bike, the act of slowing, stopping safely, grabbing my new bottle, and then getting safely back onto the road and back up to competition speed could take three or four minutes. Multiply that by the eight stops I might make in a race, and my bad arm sometimes cost me a half hour. That could be the difference between making the cutoff time and missing it and getting the dreaded DNF—Did Not Finish—next to my name.

So you can imagine my feelings of amazement, joy, and gratitude during the 2008 Ironman in Kailua-Kona when I was able to control the handlebars with my right arm, something I hadn't been able to do in twenty years. Ever since my accident in 1986 my doctors had said that I would never regain the use of my right arm. It would always be dead weight. So I accepted that medical judgment like a judge's sentence: absolute and irrefutable. I wasn't a neurosurgeon; if conventional wisdom was that my arm was out for the count, who was I to argue? Fortunately, God doesn't pay much attention to conventional wisdom.

In the 2008 Ironman World Championship, instead of pulling my bike over to drink eight or ten times, I pulled over only once. In the past, I had no confidence that if I took my left arm off the handlebars to reach for my bottle, my right arm could hold me in place. In past races I was scared of a high-speed wipeout, so I played it safe and stopped to swap out bottles. But a few minutes into the cycling stage, in the middle of the most prestigious long-distance race in the world, I decided to try taking my left hand off the handlebars. Despite using it in training, I hadn't race-tested my right arm; for all I knew I was about to go down with a first-class case of road rash. But I figured that I was in my hometown and I trained on this very road every day. I was in a comfort zone, and I knew where I was going. At that moment I didn't even feel like I was racing in the Ironman. *I think I'm going to try this* was my only thought.

I reached down with my left hand and grabbed my bottle. My right hand stayed firmly on the bars; my bike steered straight. I put the bottle back; no problem. Straight as an arrow, steady as she goes. Grinning, I started getting cute, reaching around my back with my left arm and putting things in my back pocket. The whole time I was tripping. I felt like I was being carried along by a wave of joy and blessing. I've known that sensation only one other time: during that swim in the Ultraman Canada 2009 when my legs started kicking effortlessly and I felt a current carrying me through the water like a dolphin. I felt like I wasn't in control, and I didn't care. It was a completely out-of-body experience.

Once I started drinking from the bottle, I thought, *Okay, can I get out of the saddle?* Meaning, could I stand up on the bike while ascending hills and use my body weight to pump the pedals? That's what all triathletes do, but I had never once tried it because I couldn't support myself with both arms. So in every other bike race, I had done all the hills sitting down. From a training standpoint that's not so bad because the extra work really builds up your legs; I've got quadriceps of iron now. But it's hard and slow. I knew that not being able to stand was costing me time in every race. So on a hill, I stood up. And stayed up. I was able to hold my body steady on both sides and pump with my weight. It was working! I was actually gaining speed on an uphill stretch, something I'd never done before. Best of all, standing in the saddle gave me the chance to rest my legs and back, which would keep me fresher later on.

The other competitors were pumping away like I was,

paying attention to the road. To them, I was just another rider replenishing his fluids and pounding away at the next hill. But all I could think was *There's a miracle happening, there's a miracle happening.* How could they know they had been present for one of the most significant moments of my life?

I did the rest of that Ironman riding and running on air. I finished in 13:07:21—not the kind of time I would have celebrated if I'd been able to race the way I wanted, but Coach Dave had told me that in order to have a successful Ultraman race the following month, I needed to use this day simply as a training day. More important to me was that I had used my entire body to get to the finish line. I didn't tell my team, though; I wanted to savor the private communion I was having with God and the blessing he had given me.

● ● ●

Let's be clear. I don't have full use of my arm. I still can't use it for the swim and I tuck it in my pocket for the run. But just having movement is huge. Yet this miraculous improvement didn't happen overnight. It had begun more than a year before. I was doing the Western Australia Ironman in December 2007. It was my second Ironman and notable because I hoped that finishing it would put me in a good position to be selected to do Ultraman in 2008.

The Western Australia race was run in perfect conditions, which was a relief because it can get blistering hot there. Even so, I was losing sleep over my bottle-switching dilemma. I knew my bad arm was going to cost me time. I was depressed and frustrated because my arm was holding back my performance as an athlete. But there didn't seem to be anything I could do about it.

As it turned out, I had to stop eight times during the bike stage of the race and lost about thirty minutes. Even with that handicap, I had a great race, finished, and set a personal record, beating my Arizona time by more than twenty minutes. But the thrilling development was that I felt life in my paralyzed arm. I could feel some strength returning to my arm above the elbow. No longer was it just a ten-pound lead weight grafted to my right shoulder. I could see possibilities opening before me.

Over the previous two years, all the while that I had been worrying and feeling hopeless about my racing future, God was telling me the same thing: "Just do what you're doing. Just train." Then in 2007 I went to see a chiropractor in Kona, Dr. Odin Willmott. I was there to get other parts of my body adjusted, but he asked me if he could work on my right arm. I said sure; what did I have to lose? For twenty years every doctor I went to had told me that my arm was a lost cause. The nerves had been severely damaged in the car accident and would not regenerate. I would have to live with my arm as an inert object for the rest of my life. Dr. Willmott apparently believed otherwise.

After weeks of steady manipulation and therapy by my chiropractor, the triceps muscle in my right arm actually flexed. I practically stopped breathing. I couldn't believe what I was seeing. Then the biceps moved. I starting breathing again and said silently, *God, thank you for sending another angel into my life.* Thanks to Dr. Willmott and my own relentless training, it appeared that the muscles in my arm were not dead after all. Dormant and atrophied into spaghetti, but not dead, not by a long shot.

So I continued to train and receive chiropractic therapy. Ever so slowly my arm got stronger. Over the next year I was able to use my right biceps and triceps more reliably. I gained the ability to hold my right arm steady on the handlebars rather than just anchoring it there. The more I worked, the more I was able to take my left arm off to use the bottle. In training rides I would take my left arm off my bike and see how far I could guide my bike with my right arm. I would ride for miles with only my right arm and in perfect control. It was like I had rediscovered an old friend whom I thought was lost but who for years had just been living a few streets down from me.

I was beyond excited; I was in a nearly constant state of stunned gratitude to God. *This is what you had in mind all along, didn't you?* I would say to him while I trained. He had given me the compulsion to run and cycle because doing it was healing me. Since the 2008 Ironman World Championship, other doctors have confirmed that I am getting some muscle strength and mobility back in my right arm. It's not a placebo effect; things are really regenerating. The fact that I can use my arm at all has left several doctors flabbergasted.

According to Dr. Willmott, my arm is coming back because the years of constant work—swimming, biking, and running—have been working my muscle fibers at a constant, hyperintense level, firing nerve impulses and regenerating the damaged nerves. No one told me this was possible because they didn't know it was; like me, they doubted God. More to the point, they doubted the human spirit and the limitless potential of the mind. By training so intensely for so long, I had changed my future.

It's like God has been using my Ironman training to bring my arm back. He has been giving me the strength of will and sense of purpose to train hard enough to answer my own prayer, the one I started saying years ago and probably said a thousand times: *God, if you're the god of healing and miracles, why can't you bring my arm back?* Now I know. He wasn't going to say, "Shazam!" and suddenly heal me. How would that enable me to grow or inspire others? No, God answered my prayer by showing me the way to heal *myself.*

$$\bullet \bullet \bullet$$

In the last year I've been lucky enough to speak to church groups, students, and sports teams. I hear a variation on the same question after almost every speech: "How do you do it?" Meaning, how do I motivate and push myself to handle so much pain and punishment?

When someone asks that, I give the same answer: *race for a purpose, not for yourself.* If you want to transcend your limits, get past the pain and sacrifice, and achieve goals you never thought you could achieve, find a purpose bigger than yourself in whatever you do. Following God's path inevitably takes discipline and sacrifice; there will be challenges, failure, and loss. But the journey is a lot more meaningful and joyful when you have a cause inspiring you. Finding a purpose larger than yourself allows you to expand your mental game and your physical abilities.

The difference between professional and nonprofessional athletes isn't just physical talent. It's what they do with those talents. In my case, I've trained myself to be the best athlete I can be. As grueling as that has been sometimes, it's been easier because I've learned and followed this lesson: **Get beyond yourself.**

Getting beyond yourself means finding reasons outside of your own needs and desires to push yourself. It means having a loftier purpose for training for a marathon, starting a company, writing a play, or going to medical school. Let's face it, any pursuit that is truly life altering and transformative is by definition a long, demanding, exhausting haul. If you're doing it just for yourself, it's much easier to quit when the hours become too late or your muscles get too sore. But when other people are depending on you or you have a sense of mission, you are far more likely to suck it up and keep going.

For example, a few months before the 2009 Ironman World Championship, I posted a call on my Facebook page for people to contact me who had loved ones with cancer or who had lost loved ones to cancer. Thirty-one of my Facebook friends were good enough to send me the names of the people they loved and in some cases had lost. I wore those names on the back of my jersey throughout the race, and it was like I was carrying those people's hopes and memories with me. That definitely kept me going in that grueling, hot race.

What takes you beyond yourself can be just about anything. You could do a bike race or a marathon to raise money for breast cancer or multiple sclerosis, something millions of people do every year. You could start a company and give part of your profits to a church or charity organization. You could go back to school in your fifties to inspire a member of your family who didn't finish college to return and complete her degree. What matters is that you go beyond your self-interest to find something that drives you.

I have two great purposes that push me to go beyond my limits. The first is related to the Never Stop Foundation. Ever since my car accident, I've been interested in creating facilities and programs that would help able-bodied and challenged kids realize their potential. One of the most challenging aspects of living with paralysis or other consequences of a spinal or nerve injury is maintaining hope that one day you will be able to do the things you could do before the injury. It's physically and emotionally painful to adapt to living in a wheelchair or not having the use of an arm, but eventually you do it because you have no choice. But hope is a choice; you can either maintain it or give up.

Some people, like surfer Jesse Billauer, who became a quadriplegic at seventeen when he went headfirst off his board into a sandbar, become activists. Jesse started his incredible Life Rolls On organization, which gives hope to athletes with spinal cord injuries by helping them return to the sports they love. But for millions of others, hope is hard to come by. They hear the same things from their doctors that I heard: their injuries are permanent and they will never regain any of the function they used to have. When an M.D. or Ph.D. is telling you that you'll never recover, it's pretty easy to turn your back on God and on life.

Initially, raising money for my foundation was my only broader purpose. But when I started to feel the first movement of the muscles in my arm in 2007, I realized I could do a lot more than that. I could be a living testament to hope. I could point to my right arm and say, "Look, you *can* come back. You *can* regain function. If you work hard, trust your body's natural healing power, and trust God, you can defy the predictions and get back some of what you've lost."

So when I started to feel my arm coming to life at the Western Australia Ironman in 2007, it became my purpose to be a living beacon of hope for people with neurological injuries. I found that having a larger mission behind my training and racing—doing it not just for my own glory but for the benefit of others—made a big difference in my motivation to push through the pain and keep going. Every time a newspaper or TV station does a story about me, they mention my paralyzed arm. These days, they also mention the fact that my arm is coming back. I imagine a few people living with their own injuries seeing those stories and thinking, *Wow! Maybe if that guy can heal his injury through discipline and hard work, so can I!* If I can inspire just a few children or adults to say, "I don't accept this," and discover the strength to do things they didn't think they could, then my purpose will be fulfilled.

I envision a "circle of inspiration": a handful of folks with spinal cord injuries motivated by what I'm doing, changing their lives, and in turn inspiring more people to do the same, and on and on. What starts with one or two or five people could become one hundred or one thousand or one million, like the ripples in a pond expanding outward. What a blessing that would be to the world!

● ● ●

Most of us are wired the same way: we find it relatively easy to accept our own failures, but we imagine that those same failures are intolerable to other people. So when we're doing something long and arduous and we feel like we can't go on anymore, it can be easy to slack off and say, "You know, I'm beat. I'm going to give myself a break and get back to this tomorrow." It's different when you imagine your children, your friends, or a bunch of kids in wheelchairs watching you quit and being disappointed in you. That's almost impossible to bear. We're willing to let ourselves down sometimes, but it's much tougher to dash somebody else's hopes. Use that to your advantage. Find a purpose or a cause bigger than yourself, and dedicate yourself to serving that purpose as you go after what you want. With the right motivation, the mind has incredible power to push the body to places it doesn't really want to go.

Why do you think so many elderly and terminally ill people manage to stay alive for Christmas and the New Year? They cherish those holidays—the family, the celebrations—and their anticipation gives them a purpose, which is to enjoy those wonderful times for one more year. Once that purpose is past, they often slip away very quickly.

Or what about Doris Haddock, otherwise known as Granny D? She was a retired office assistant in New Hampshire until her husband died when she was ninety. Needing a reason to keep going, she (and this still blows me away) decided to walk across America to rally people against the influence of big money in elections. At ninety years old. Most people at ninety can barely walk across a room. Four years later she ran for the Senate and almost won. She's been the subject of a documentary, *Run Granny Run,* and she celebrated her ninety-ninth birthday last year at the New Hampshire State House, lobbying for campaign finance reform. Talk about motivated by a purpose!

However, there is another, even stronger purpose that keeps me pushing: my relationship with God. I'm blessed enough to be doing these things—writing this book, making a documentary, competing against the best distance athletes on the planet—because I finally paid attention to the path God had been showing me for years. I owe everything I am to his love and his incredible vision for me. So now, when I compete, I'm also doing it to proclaim how incredible God is—to be living testimony to his power to transform our lives.

What purpose could keep you going toward the thing you want most? Is there something that you dream about, some incredible life goal that you tried to achieve when you were younger but gave up on because you got distracted or the road just seemed too steep? That's your calling. That passion is God talking to you, telling you, "This is your destiny." Whatever it is, if you really want to pursue it and make it a reality, you can. Find a larger purpose beyond your own interest. Serve someone or something else with what you do.

If you've always wanted to run a marathon, run for a charity that has personal meaning for you. If you're launching a company, hire underprivileged kids from the neighborhood. If you're trying to lose weight, find sponsors who will donate money to your old high school for every pound you drop. If you've always wanted to write a book, write one that tells the stories of elders in your church so that they will be counting on you to finish. Put something meaningful on the line—jobs, needed funds, people's hopes—and make its success hinge on whether you succeed or fail.

Or if you're incredibly blessed, as I've been, make God your purpose. If he's transformed your life, promise him that you'll beat the odds, and refuse to lose. Show the world what he can do when we open our eyes and hearts to him.

Study Guide for Church and Bible Study Groups

I hope that my story has raised as many questions for you as it has answered. I hope it has encouraged you to look at the twists and turns of your own life to uncover the lessons that the Lord is trying to teach every one of us. I encourage my readers to join in fellowship with members of their churches, in Bible study groups, or in private gatherings to discuss *Running on Faith* and how what I have shared with you can help you discover God's deeper purpose in your own journey. To that end, I have put together this brief collection of questions and study suggestions. Use them in groups or even in your personal time of prayer and reflection to discover the doors that our Lord is holding open, waiting for you to walk through.

—*Jason*

1. Can you recall a time when God revealed his broader purpose for you? How did you react? How would you react now after reading Jason's story?

2. We have all lost something in our lives—loved ones, jobs, opportunities. Can you look back and see how a loss was really a gateway to a new stage of life's race?

3. Why do you think God allows suffering and loss in our lives, as he did with Jason? What purpose could it serve?

4. Where does a person's responsibility to family end and his or her responsibility to follow the purpose of God begin? Have you ever struggled with that balance?

5. Jason finds time to commune with God in the midst of his races. When do you feel most in communion with God and why?

6. What sort of Laboratory could you create in order to help you draw closer to achieving your highest goals?

7. What meaning lies behind the healing of Jason's right arm?

8. How do we know when God is holding open a door for us to walk through? Why doesn't he simply push us through?

9. Do those who pray ask for God's intervention or for God to bring them the wisdom and strength to do his will? If neither one, what do they pray for?

10. What pattern of events do you see unfolding in your own past, and what does it reveal to you about the purpose God has in mind for you?

11. Why might triathletes as a group be so strongly spiritual?

12. Why does a greater purpose help drive many athletes and other achievers to do far more than if they were only out for themselves?

13. How do you think God reveals his intent to us? Visions? Words? Signs? What else?

14. How do you and those you know "put God in a box," that is, put limits on what you think God can achieve in your life?

Ultranutrition

In 2009 I became a vegan, which means I don't eat anything made from animal products, including dairy and eggs. I've gotten some attention from the triathlete community for this, and I have my share of doubters. Many people think that unless I eat animal products, I can't get enough protein to fuel my body and heal the muscle damage that occurs when I race. But that's simply not true.

By eating a broad selection of high-protein plant-based foods—including nut butters, tofu, tempeh, and beans—I get all the protein I need while getting an incredible rush of nutrients and fiber that are critical to my health and performance. The fact is, since going from vegetarian to vegan, I've found that my energy level is incredible and my recovery time is even shorter than when I was eating animal products. The vegan diet helped me finish eighteenth among thirty-six competitors and break the thirty-hour mark in the 2009 Ultraman World Championship in Kailua-Kona.

You don't have to go vegan if you want to compete in Ironman triathlons (or any other races), but there are certain nutritional rules you should follow if you want to perform at your optimal level, have incredible energy, stay healthy, and feel your best before, during, and after races:

DO

- Consume huge amounts of fresh fruits, vegetables, beans, and herbs—no limits

- Eat healthy amounts of nuts, seeds, and almond butter (in moderation because they are high in calories)

- Eat lots of lean protein, such as tofu, seitan, and tempeh

- If you feel the need to eat meat, stick to fish

- Eat plenty of complex carbohydrates, such as brown rice, hemp bread, and sprouted pasta

- Drink plenty of water

- Eat lots of healthy fats from sources like avocados, virgin coconut oil, and coconut meat

- Eat organic foods whenever possible

- If you must use sweetener, use agave syrup

DON'T

- Eat red meat

- Drink alcohol, which dehydrates you

- Eat processed foods

- Consume anything "white": flour, rice, potatoes, bread

- Consume anything with high fructose corn syrup

These rules might seem strict, but once you've spent some time following them, and you see how incredible this way of eating makes you feel and how much better you perform athletically, it will become easy to eat this way every day.

VEGAN RECIPES

These are some of my favorite vegan recipes, taken from the book *Jai Ultra/Seed Plant-Based Whole Food Cookbook,* by Ananda Shreemanti and Richard Roll, available at www.richroll.com.

Arugula Spring Salad

This is a hearty, crunchy salad full of flavor. Serve alone or with a soup entrée and banana scones.

½ cup chopped organic celery

1 organic carrot, sliced

¼ organic red pepper, diced

2 cups organic arugula

2 ripe organic figs, quartered

½ organic avocado, seeded, peeled, and diced

½ organic tomato, quartered

2 tbsp organic almonds, slivered

DRESSING

2 tbsp organic olive oil

1 tsp fine Celtic sea salt

Juice of ¼ organic lemon

Splash of organic apple cider vinegar

In a medium bowl, add dressing ingredients. Add celery, carrots, pepper. Toss to coat. Add arugula, figs, avocado, tomatoes, and almonds. Toss and serve.

Asian Salad

¼ cup sesame oil
¼ cup organic soy sauce
Juice of 1 small lime
⅛ tsp black pepper
One 2.1-oz package sea vegetables
1 cup spring lettuce mix
1 cup sprouted mung beans
1 cup daikon sprouts (or substitute any kind of sprouts)
1 tbsp black sesame seeds

In a serving salad bowl, mix the sesame oil, soy sauce, the juice of the lime, and pepper. Add the sea vegetables and stir to coat. Add the lettuce, mung beans, and daikon sprouts. Toss and sprinkle with sesame seeds.

Chia Seed Pudding

This is a raw vegan pudding that is great brain food. Chia seeds are known to be the "runner" food of the Aztecs. They are packed with protein. Enjoy!

8 tbsp chia seeds (black)
2 cups filtered water
2 tbsp raw honey

1 medium avocado, seeded and peeled

2 tbsp raw cacao powder

2 tbsp organic coconut oil

Put chia seeds in a small bowl with filtered water. Stir for three to five minutes until they become gelatinous. In a food processor, add chia seed and water mixture, honey, avocado, cacao powder, and coconut oil. Process for 3 minutes, stopping to scrape down the sides of the bowl. Adjust honey and cocoa powder to taste. Pour into individual serving bowls and chill. Serve cold.

Fluffy Mousse Shake

½ banana, peeled

2 tbsp chia seeds

2 tbsp lecithin granules

Juice of 1 organic grapefruit

1 organic orange

½ organic lemon

1 tbsp organic coconut oil

5 tbsp organic agave or raw honey

1 tsp vanilla extract

¼ cup filtered water

Crushed ice

Place all ingredients in a blender and blend for one minute or until smooth. Makes 2 large shakes.

Glazed Figs with Manuka Honey

Manuka honey is being called the cure-all food. You can find it in various qualities at Whole Foods. I treat it like caviar and splurge on the best I can find.

15 large ripe black figs
Organic coconut oil
1 jar high-quality Manuka honey

Slice the figs in half and place face up on a lightly oiled (use coconut oil) cookie sheet. Place in the oven at 375° F for ten minutes or until glazed.

Place a few on a serving plate and drizzle 1 teaspoon of Manuka honey on top.

You can add some toasted pineolas and some fresh chopped mint if you like. Or serve them alongside the Chia Seed Pudding (see p. 164).

Grilled Tofu

1 lb organic tofu
¼ cup Japanese rice vinegar
Sea salt
Ground black pepper to taste
⅛ cup lemon juice
½ cup Nama Shoyu soy sauce (raw, unpasteurized)
⅛ cup organic olive oil
Large bunch of spinach (triple what you think you need, since it reduces down drastically)
⅛ cup organic sesame oil

1 tbsp black sesame seeds

1 cup short-grain brown rice, cooked

Slice tofu into cross sections first to make three thin rectangles. Then slice those twice so you have three pieces of each section. Marinate the tofu in a deep dish, adding the rice vinegar, salt, pepper, lemon juice, and Nama Shoyu. Set aside.

In a large wok, heat olive oil. Add spinach and sauté until just limp. Transfer to serving platter. Add sesame oil and place tofu filets carefully to fit inside the wok. Some pieces will move up the side of the wok. Brown well, then turn and repeat. In the last minute of browning on the flip side, add marinade and reduce for three minutes. Using a metal spatula, lift the filets out of the wok and arrange on top of the spinach. Pour remaining marinade over the tofu filets. Sprinkle with sesame seeds and drizzle with Nama Shoyu. Serve with short-grain brown rice.

Guacamole

This is the tastiest guacamole ever. It is simple and free of spicy ingredients. The kids love this one! Serve with chips and salsa or mound it on top of nachos.

4 ripe organic avocados, seeded and peeled

Juice of 1 medium lemon

Celtic sea salt

On a plate, cut avocado crosswise to make small cubes. Squeeze the lemon juice over the avocado and add sea salt. Continue cutting until everything is mixed well. Adjust salt and lemon to taste.

Mushroom Gravy

¼ onion, peeled and sliced

Organic olive oil

1 portobello mushroom

4 small bunches shelf, shitake, porcini, and/or any fresh
     local mushrooms

¼ cup arrowroot powder

2 cups filtered water

3 tbsp Nama Shoyu soy sauce

2 tsp sea salt or ¼ cup kalamata olives, pitted

1 sprig fresh rosemary

2 fresh sage leaves

In a large saucepan, brown the onion in some olive oil.
Add the portobello and other mushrooms. Sauté for five minutes until the juices come out. Whisk the arrowroot powder in
a cup of filtered water and add to the mushrooms. Stir until it
thickens. Add the soy sauce, salt *or* olives, and herbs.

Pour the mushroom mixture into a blender and blend,
adding more water to make desired consistency. Adjust salt
to taste. If you wait to pour the mixture into the blender
until just before serving, it will heat the gravy for you. Blend-
ing takes roughly 3 minutes.

Sprouted Lentils or Mung Beans

2 tbsp organic olive oil

1 celery stalk with leaves, chopped

2 carrots, diced

2 cups fresh sprouted lentils or mung beans

4 cups filtered water

1 tsp or more Celtic sea salt

½ tsp turmeric, freshly grated or powder

½ tsp cumin seeds or powder

1 tbsp Nama Shoyu soy sauce

½ small lemon

Fresh cilantro

In a large pot, heat the olive oil, then add the celery. Sauté until the color brightens. Add the carrots and sauté again for five minutes. Add the fresh sprouted lentils or mung beans. Sauté to coat. Add water and bring to a boil for five minutes. Reduce heat to a simmer. When the water reduces down, add spices and Nama Shoyu to taste. Add a squeeze of half a small lemon and fresh cilantro just before serving.

Vegan Potato Salad

1 large bag organic potatoes (You can use small red potatoes or Yukon Gold and leave the skins on. If you use russet, you'll need to rub the skins off after they are done.)

1½ cups Vegenaise (This is a vegan mayonnaise you can find at Whole Foods in the refrigerated section. There are a few types; get the one that has grapeseed oil if possible. It's a great natural antibiotic.)

½ cup organic olive oil

½ cup Bubbies relish (This is a probiotic relish that has no

vinegar, sugar, or preservatives; you can find it at Whole
Foods.)

¼ cup fresh dill

Celtic (or great quality) sea salt to taste

Ground black pepper

Wash the potatoes and boil them in water until tender.
Transfer them into a colander and drain the water off. Cut
the potatoes crosswise into small cubes. In a serving bowl,
combine potatoes, Vegenaise, olive oil, relish, dill, and sea
salt and pepper. Use salt and pepper to taste.

PERFORMANCE AND RECOVERY BLENDS

These are great performance drinks—the first two to get
you fired up for the morning training session, the second
two to help you recover from the day's training. Just mix all
the ingredients and blend. Drink immediately.

Performance Blends

RECIPE ONE

1 cup organic pineapple, skin removed (fresh, if possible)

1 large leaf organic kale

2 tbsp maca root powder

2 tbsp chia seeds

½ cup organic raw shaved coconut

2 tbsp organic coconut oil

1 cup organic orange juice

RECIPE TWO

1 medium organic beet, raw, unpeeled

1 small organic apple, cored, unpeeled

1 stalk organic celery, with leaves

1 large organic kale leaf

2 tbsp maca root powder

2 tbsp hemp seed

2 tbsp flax oil

1 tbsp blue-green algae

1 cup organic apple juice

Recovery Blends

RECIPE ONE

1 organic banana, peeled

1 handful organic almonds

2 tbsp rice protein

2 tbsp raw cacao

2 tbsp raw honey

½ organic avocado, seeded and peeled

1 cup organic coconut milk

RECIPE TWO

1 stalk red chard

1 handful organic pumpkin seeds

1 sheet raw seaweed (nori, dulse, or sea lettuce)

½ organic red bell pepper (discard seeds and stem)

½ organic avocado, seeded and peeled

1 small organic lemon, rind removed

1 tbsp Celtic sea salt

1 cup filtered water

So You Want to Train for an Ironman?

People all around the world compete in triathlons each year. It is something that almost anyone can do with the right guidance, sound training, good nutritional strategies, and of course an iron sense of discipline. If after reading my story you're interested in learning more about training to compete in an Ironman-length triathlon, I encourage you to learn more. There may not be a better feeling in the world than knowing you've achieved something that many people will never even attempt. It feels even better to race because you're in the center of God's purpose.

So if you feel that God is calling you to your own Ironman journey, here are some tips on beginning your own Ironman training, followed by my personal twelve-week training regimen:

- It's helpful to know how your body responds to extreme distance racing, so before you think about trying an Ironman, first try doing some 10K races, half marathons, marathons, and even biathlons. You'll learn volumes about everything from hydration and recovery to lactate thresholds and injury prevention.

- Find a good coach. The best professionals in every field in the world have coaches or mentors. Why? Because you can't be objective about your own performance. You need someone to be brutally honest about your weaknesses and to devise a plan to help you improve. A good coach will become your best friend as you head for an Ironman starting line.

- Talk to your doctor. Before you embark on something as outrageous as trying a triathlon, get a full physical to make sure you don't have any underlying cardiac, joint, or other health conditions that might make it dangerous to compete.

- Find a community of triathletes in your area. I know I've said this is a very selfish sport, but beginning triathletes are incredibly supportive because you're going through the same pain and struggle they are. Get online or go to a local running club and talk to people who are working toward the same goal you're chasing. You'll find good advice, swap stories, and maybe find a second family who will be with you when you hit rough spots on the racecourse.

- Start slow. Don't try to run a marathon the first day out, even if you've run one before. As you'll see in my training guide, training for an Ironman triathlon is like training for nothing else. Go easy on yourself, listen to your body, get plenty of rest, and persevere. If it takes you fifty-two weeks instead of twelve to be ready for your first Ironman, you know what? The race will still be there, waiting.

- Finally, find a purpose larger than yourself to serve. Race for a charity or in memory of someone you loved. Find something bigger than your own ego to keep you going when your body wants to give in to the pain. Because there will be pain and heat and suffering. It's not easy. But when you do it, you will feel God by your side.

Here's the training plan that I use:

SUMMIT PERFORMANCE COACHING: 24-WEEK IRONMAN TRAINING PROGRAM BY COACH DAVID CIAVERELLA

There are many types of athletes: those with pure physical gifts, those with marginal physical ability, and those with below-average physical ability. But athletes also come in different psychological packages: those with incredible will, those with a moderate competitive spirit, and the ones who complete endurance events to "check it off the list." Endurance athletes bear many combinations of these characteristics. But the great ones have something extra that allows them to go far beyond what they seem capable of in a race situation. Instead of surrendering to pain and despair at a critical moment in a race, they embrace it. Rather than worry about not succeeding, they accept the challenge willingly and invite the outcome, whatever it is. I don't know if that's something that can be learned or coached, but I have found it just comes naturally to some athletes. It has nothing to do with physical ability, but it enhances performance beyond the mere potential of the athlete's physiology.

Jason Lester has it. We've never discussed it. I have never asked Jason *why*. I do not have to. I know *why* he does this as simply as I know why I do it, my wife Ann does it, and a host of others around the planet do it. You hear about "lifetime base" a great deal when it comes to endurance events. What many athletes and coaches do not realize is that this does not necessarily imply a physical state, but a psychological and emotional state that is a precursor to success. This is how Jason wills himself to the finish line despite the odds against him. He has that secret to success that many others cannot seem to find.

Training prepares us to reach that defining moment in an endurance race. The state of isolation we enter, when we are physically stripped of everything and left with the bare emotional state of purity, is the point of enlightenment. Getting to this defining moment, and rising above it, is what we train for. Our *why* is what drives us. Jason has found his *why,* and through his life is showing others that nearly anything is possible.

—*David Ciaverella*

This program assumes base fitness before starting and assumes that the athlete is not using a wattage power meter or focusing on heart rate. The program begins with several base building weeks then moves to a series of build weeks with periodic recovery weeks. These build into the pretaper and taper phases, which are the week before and the week of the race. This program is for general guidance only and is as suggested by Coach David Cia-

verella. It is not intended to represent high-level coaching or personalized coaching, both of which make significantly more contributions to the individual athlete. Summit Performance Coaching (www.summitpc.net) and its coaches make no claims about outcomes of prewritten training programs such as this, which do not include the supervision of a physician and a dedicated coach. Pace suggestions are generalizations based on athletes' projections of their goals and do not imply that athletes are capable of achieving those goals. Users of this training guide determine their own pace and effort as they prepare to complete their first Ironman distance triathlon. Any person engaging in a training program in physical fitness should consult a licensed physician prior to initiating that program. Triathlon, and in particular Ironman-distance triathlon, involves a significant amount of physical and psychological stamina and subsequent risk of injury. Routine consultation with a physician and personal coach is advised during any such program.

GLOSSARY

12 x 50/15 drill 25, freestyle 25. 8 x 25/10 kickboard: *12 intervals of 50 yards with 15 seconds' rest between, choose your stroke for 25 yards, freestyle for 25 yards, 8 intervals of 25 yards on the kickboard with 10 seconds' rest between*

brick: *training on two disciplines during the same workout*

cadence: *rpm in cycling or running*

catch-up drill: *freestyle swim where you don't pull until your hands are together in front of you*

descend: *each interval is faster than the last*

first 6 sprint 12 strokes during first 25 yards: *first 6 intervals, you sprint, like at the start of a race, for the first 12 strokes*

fist drill: *freestyle with hands in fists*

Olympic tri pace: *the pace you would use if you were competing in an Olympic-length triathlon, 1.5K swim, 40K ride, 10K run*

pull: *freestyle swimming stroke, pulling the arm downward through the water along the center line of the body.*

sprint tri effort: *the effort you would use if racing in a sprint-distance triathlon*

Week 1 = Base	Week 9 = Build	Week 17 = Build
Week 2 = Base	Week 10 = Build	Week 18 = Build
Week 3 = Base	Week 11 = Recovery	Week 19 = Recovery
Week 4 = Base	Week 12 = Build	Week 20 = Build
Week 5 = Base	Week 13 = Build	Week 21 = Build
Week 6 = Base	Week 14 = Build	Week 22 = Build
Week 7 = Build	Week 15 = Recovery	Week 23 = Pretaper
Week 8 = Recovery	Week 16 = Build	Week 24 = Taper
		(Race Week)

WEEK 1 (BASE)

M   Swim A.M. or P.M.: 1,600 (all swim distances are in yards)
400 pull easy. 12 x 50/15 drill 25, freestyle 25. 8 x 25/10 kickboard. 400 pull easy.
Weights after swim: legs 30 minutes, keep weight light; focus on 20 reps and 2–3 sets.

T   Bike A.M. or P.M.: 18 miles or 50 minutes on trainer, easy pace.
Run A.M. or P.M.: 4 miles, run easy and keep separate from bike.

W Swim A.M.: 1,600

300 pull easy. 16 x 50/15 steady on all. 100 easy pull recovery. 400 easy freestyle.

Run P.M.: 6 miles, easy pace.

T Bike P.M.: 22 miles or 60 minutes on trainer, easy and steady.

F Swim A.M. or P.M.: 1,600

4 x 400/30 (1 = 400 free, 2 = 2 x 200/20, 3 = 400 pull, 4 = 4 x 100/15).

Weights after swim: legs 30 minutes, keep weight light, focus on 20 reps and 2–3 sets.

S Bike A.M.: 35 miles, steady easy ride, rolling hills.

S Run A.M.: 8 miles, easy, even splits.

WEEK 2 (BASE)

M Swim A.M. or P.M.: 1,600

400 pull easy. 12 x 50/15 drill 25, freestyle 25. 8 x 25/10 kickboard. 400 pull easy.

Weights after swim: legs 30 minutes, keep weight light, focus on 20 reps and 2–3 sets.

T Bike: A.M. or P.M.: 18 miles, or 50 minutes on trainer, easy pace.

Run A.M. or P.M.: 6 miles, easy, and keep separate from bike.

W Swim A.M. or P.M.: 1,600

300 pull easy. 16 x 50/15 steady on all. 100 easy pull recovery. 400 easy freestyle.

Run A.M. or P.M., can run after swim: 6 miles, run easy.

T Bike P.M.: 25 miles, steady easy ride or 70 minutes on trainer.

F Swim A.M.: 2,000

4 x 500/30 (1 = 500 free, 2 = 5 x 100/15, 3 = 500 pull, 4 = 10 x 50/10)

Run P.M.: 4 miles on treadmill before weights, 0% incline, easy steady pace.

Weights after run: legs 30 minutes, keep weight light, focus on 20 reps and 2–3 sets

S   Bike A.M.: 35 miles, steady easy ride, rolling hills.

S   Run A.M.: 8 miles, easy, even splits.

WEEK 3 (BASE)

M   Swim A.M. or P.M.: 2,000

500 pull easy. 6 x 50/15 drill 25, freestyle 25. 6 x 100/20 steady. 8 x 25/10 kickboard. 400 pull easy.

Run P.M.: 4 miles easy treadmill before weights, 0% incline and easy steady pace.

Weights after run: legs 30 minutes, keep weight light, focus on 20 reps and 2–3 sets.

T   Bike A.M. or P.M.: 22 miles or 60 minutes on trainer. Steady pace, comfortable.

Run 2 miles brick off bike. Keep easy.

W   Swim A.M.: 1,600

400 pull easy. 12 x 75/15 steady on all. 300 steady free.

Run P.M.: 6 miles, rolling hills.

T   Bike P.M.: 25 miles, steady easy ride or 70 minutes on trainer.

F   Swim A.M.: 2,000

4 x 500/30 (1 = 500 free, 2 = 5 x 100/15, 3 = 500 pull, 4 = 10 x 50/10)

Run P.M.: 4 miles on treadmill before weights, 0% incline, easy steady pace.

Weights after run: legs 30 minutes, keep weight light, focus on 20 reps and 2–3 sets.

S   Bike A.M.: 35 miles, steady easy ride, rolling hills.

Run P.M.: 3 miles, keep separate from bike, run easy.

S   Run A.M.: 8 miles, easy, even splits.

WEEK 4 (BASE)

M Swim A.M. or P.M.: 2,000

500 pull easy. 6 x 50/15 drill 25, freestyle 25. 4 x 150/20 steady. 8 x 25/10 kickboard. 400 pull easy.

Weights after swim: legs 30 minutes, keep weight light, focus on 20 reps and 2–3 sets.

T Bike A.M. or P.M.: 22 miles or 60 minutes on trainer. Steady pace, comfortable.

Run A.M. or P.M.: 6 miles, keep separate from bike.

W Swim A.M.: 1,600

400 pull easy. 6 x 100/20. Descend 1–3, then repeat 4–6. 600 steady free.

Run P.M.: 8 miles, rolling hills.

T Bike P.M.: 30 miles, steady easy ride, rolling hills, or 80 minutes on trainer.

F Swim A.M.: 2,500

5 x 500/30 (1 = 500 free, 2 = 2 x 250/30, 3 = 500 pull, 4 = 5 x 100/15, 5 = 500 free)

Weights after swim: legs 30 minutes, keep weight light, focus on 20 reps and 2–3 sets.

S Bike A.M.: 45 miles, steady easy ride, rolling hills.

S Run A.M.: 12 miles, keep run slow.

WEEK 5 (BASE)

M Swim A.M. or P.M.: 2,500

500 pull easy. 4 x 25/10 kick. 12 x 75/20 steady, break up into 3 sets of 4, and for each set choose a different drill for the middle 25 of each 75. 8 x 100/15 all steady and even. 200 pull easy.

Weights after swim: legs 30 minutes, keep weight light, focus on 20 reps and 2–3 sets.

T Bike A.M.: 45 minutes on trainer. 20 minutes steady, then 12 x 30 second single leg (6 each leg) at low cadence of

50 rpm. Start on 1-minute cycles to allow time to
unclip and change legs. Steady after.

Run P.M.: 4 miles, easy, steady run.

W Swim A.M.: 2,000

500 easy. 3 x 200/30 descend each. 100 pull slow recovery.
4 x 100/20 descend each. 400 pull easy.

Run P.M.: 6 miles, easy, no hills.

T Bike P.M.: 22 miles, steady easy ride, rolling hills, try to keep
heart rate down on uphills by lowering cadence to 50.

F Swim A.M. or P.M.: 2,500

5 x 500/30 (1 = 500 free, 2 = 2 x 250/30, 3 = 500 pull, 4 = 5
x 100/15, 5 = 500 free).

Weights after swim: legs 30 minutes, keep weight light,
focus on 20 reps and 2–3 sets.

S Bike A.M.: 50 miles, steady easy ride, rolling hills, lower
cadence to 50 on uphills.

S Run A.M.: 12 miles, keep run easy, can run slightly faster
than last week if comfortable.

WEEK 6 (BASE)

M Bike A.M.: 40 minutes on trainer. 20 minutes steady. Then
12 x 30 second single leg (6 each) like last week, hold
cadence at 50 on each, and start on 1-minute cycles.

Swim P.M.: 3,000

500 pull easy. 2 sets (2 x 200/30 + 4 x 100/20 + 4 x 50/10).
Second set all faster. 400 pull easy.

Weights after swim: legs 30 minutes, keep weight light,
focus on 20 reps and 2–3 sets.

T Run A.M.: 4 miles, easy steady pace.

Bike P.M.: 22 miles, steady comfortable pace.

W Swim A.M.: 1,600

400 pull easy. 16 x 50/10 all steady and even pace. 400 pull
easy.

Run A.M. + P.M.: 3 miles course run + 6. 3 miles on treadmill after A.M. swim, easy, 0% incline. P.M.: 6 miles, rolling hills.

T Bike A.M.: 40 minutes on trainer, steady comfortable pace.
Bike P.M.: 25 miles, rolling hills. Lower cadence to about 50 on uphills to control heart rate.

F Swim A.M. or P.M.: 3,000
5 x 600/30 (1 = 600 free, steady pace, 2 = 3 x 200/30, 3 = 600 pull, slow, 4 = 6 x 100/15 even, 5 = 600 free, steady pace).
Weights after swim: legs 30 minutes, keep weight light, focus on 20 reps and 2–3 sets.

S Bike A.M.: 50 miles, steady easy ride, rolling hills, lower cadence to 50 on uphills.
Run A.M.: 3 miles, brick off bike, keep pace easy.

S Run A.M.: 14 miles, keep run easy.

WEEK 7 (BUILD)

M Bike A.M.: 40 minutes on trainer. 20 minutes steady. Then 16 x 30 second single leg (8 each) like last week, hold cadence at 50 on each, and start on 1-minute cycles.
Swim P.M.: 3,000
500 pull easy. 2 sets (2 x 200/30 + 4 x 100/20 + 4 x 50/10). Second set all faster. 400 pull easy.

T Run A.M.: 5 miles, easy steady pace.
Bike P.M.: 20 miles, steady comfortable base pace. After 20 minutes, work in 3 x 5 minute intervals sprint tri effort, and focus on holding cadence at 80–90 by using higher gear. Take 5-minute easy spin rest between each.

W Swim A.M.: 1,600
400 pull easy. 16 x 50/10 all steady and even pace. 400 pull easy.

Run P.M.: 7 miles. After 2 miles slow, do 5 x 2 minute
intervals at 5K–10K run pace. Take 3-minute recovery
slow run between each.

T Bike A.M.: 40 minutes on trainer, steady comfortable pace.
Bike P.M.: 25 miles, rolling hills. Lower cadence to about
50 on uphills to control heart rate.

F Swim A.M. or P.M.: 3,000
5 x 600/30 (1 = 600 free, steady pace, 2 = 3 x 200/30,
3 = 600 pull, slow, 4 = 6 x 100/15 even, 5 = 600 free,
steady pace).
Run A.M. or P.M.: 4 miles, easy recovery. Can run after
swim or separate.

S Bike A.M.: 65 miles, steady easy ride.

S Run A.M.: 16 miles, keep run easy.

WEEK 8 (RECOVERY)

M Day off.

T Swim A.M.: 3,000
600 steady. 3 sets (3 x 100/20 descend + 6 x 50/10 even + 4
x 25/10 kickboard). 300 pull easy.

W Swim A.M.: 1,600. Swim continuous, steady.
Run P.M.: 7 miles. Work in 5 x 1 minute, 5K-pace intervals
during run, 1 per mile after 2-mile warm up. Base
pace is Ironman marathon (IM) goal pace.

T Bike A.M. or P.M.: 25 miles, comfortable easy pace, work in
a few rolling hills, cadence at 50 on uphills.

F Run A.M.: 5 miles, easy, steady.
Swim P.M.: 3,000
5 x 600/30 (1 = 600 free, steady pace, 2 = 3 x 200/30, 3 =
600 pull, slow, 4 = 3 x 200/20, 5 = 600 free, steady
pace).

S Bike A.M.: 65 miles, easy steady ride.

S Run A.M.: 12 miles, easy steady run.

WEEK 9 (BUILD)

M Swim P.M.: 3,500

800 easy. Work in choice drill on first 25 of each 100. Then 2 sets (3 x 200/20 + 4 x 100/15 + 4 x 50/10) all steady strong pace. 1-minute rest between sets. 500 easy pull.

Bike A.M.: 40 minutes, steady and comfortable. After 20 minutes, work in 16 x 30 second single leg (8 each), cadence at 50 on each. Start on 1-minute cycles.

T Run A.M.: 4 miles, easy even pace.

Bike P.M.: 25 miles, steady comfortable pace.

Run P.M.: 2 mile brick off bike. 2 minutes slow. Then run IM goal pace.

W Swim A.M.: 1,600

400 pull easy. 20 x 50/10, all steady and even pace. 200 pull easy.

Run P.M.: 7 miles, comfortable steady run, work up to IM goal pace.

T Swim A.M.: 1,600. Continuous easy and even pace.

Bike P.M.: 35 miles, rolling hills. Lower cadence to 50 on all uphills.

F Swim P.M.: 3,000

800 easy. Work in choice drill, first 25 of each 100. 6 x 200/20 easy and steady, and for each, work in a 12-stroke sprint first 25. 8 x 25/10 kickboard. 6 x 100/30 steady, and for each, work in a 12-stroke sprint final 25. 400 pull slow.

Run P.M.: 4 miles, easy, after swim.

S Bike A.M.: 80 miles, steady comfortable ride.

S Run A.M.: 14 miles, 30 seconds slower than IM goal first 6 miles. Then IM goal pace final 8 miles.

WEEK 10 (BUILD)

M   Swim A.M. or P.M.: 3,500
    800 easy. Work in choice drill on first 25 of each 100. Then
    2 sets (3 x 200/20 + 4 x 100/15 + 4 x 50/10) all steady
    strong pace. 1-minute rest between sets. 500 easy pull.

T   Run A.M.: 6 miles, easy even pace.
    Bike P.M.: 25 miles. After 30 minutes easy, 4 x 5 minute
    intervals at Olympic tri pace with cadence target in 80s
    using higher gear. 3-minute easy recovery between
    each. Steady pace after to end.

W   Swim A.M.: 1,600
    400 pull easy. 10 x 100/15, steady and even pace. Choice
    drill, first 25 on all 100s. 200 pull easy.
    Run P.M.: 8 miles. 2-mile slow warm-up. Then 5 x 3
    minutes at 5K–10K pace with 3-minute easy recovery
    between each. After, run IM goal pace to end of run.

T   Bike P.M.: 35 miles, rolling hills. Lower cadence to 50 on
    all uphills.

F   Swim P.M.: 4,000
    5 x 800 (1 = 800 free, 2 = 4 x 200/30 steady, 3 = 800 pull
    easy, 4 = 8 x 100/20 steady, 5 = 800 free like first one).
    Run P.M.: 5 miles, easy after swim or separate from swim
    in A.M.

S   Bike A.M.: 60 miles, steady, comfortable ride.
    Run A.M.: 3 miles brick off bike. 5 minutes, 30 seconds
    slower than IM goal pace. Then run IM goal pace
    remainder of run.

S   Run A.M.: 18 miles. 30 seconds slower than IM goal first 6
    miles. Then IM goal pace final 12 miles.

WEEK 11 (RECOVERY)

M   Day off.
T   Swim A.M.: 3,200

600 easy pull. 3 x 200/30 descend each. 6 x 150/20 middle
50 choice drill on each. 12 x 75/15 first 6 sprint 12
strokes first 25. Final 6 sprint 12 strokes final 25.
Bike p.m.: 25 miles, comfortable steady ride.

W Swim a.m.: 2,000
4 x 500/30. All are steady, and try to slightly descend each one.
Run p.m.: 6 miles. 2 miles 30 seconds slower then IM pace.
4 miles 30 seconds faster than IM goal pace.

T Bike p.m.: 35 miles. After 45 minutes easy, work in 2 x 8
minute intervals at Olympic tri pace with cadence
75–85. Easy and comfortable pace after to end.

F Swim p.m.: 4,000
5 x 800 (1 = 800 free, 2 = 4 x 200/30 steady, 3 = 800 pull
easy, 4 = 8 x 100/20 steady, 5 = 800 free like first one).
Run p.m.: 4 miles easy after swim or separate from swim
in a.m. Final mile work in 4 x 20 second strides. Not
sprinting, just about 5K race pace for strides.

S Bike a.m.: 65 miles, steady comfortable ride.
Run p.m.: 4 miles. Start slow 5–10 minutes, then run IM goal
pace remainder. No brick, keep run separate from bike.

S Run a.m.: 18 miles. 30 seconds slower than IM goal first 6
miles. Then IM goal pace final 12 miles.

WEEK 12 (BUILD)

M Swim a.m. or p.m.: 3,600 pyramid. 30 seconds rest between
everything.
100–200–300–400–500–600–500–400–300–200–100.
Start comfortable, and swim slightly faster on the
second half of the set.

T Run a.m.: 5 miles, easy recovery run.
Bike p.m.: 25 miles. After 20 minutes easy, 3 x 8 minute
intervals at Olympic tri pace with cadence target at 75
using higher gear. 4 minutes easy recovery between
each. Steady pace after to end.

W   Swim A.M.: 2,000

    800 free, steady comfortable. 4 x 50/10 kickboard. 5 x 200/20 catch-up drill first 50 of each.

    Run P.M.: 7 miles. Run 15 seconds to 30 seconds faster than IM goal pace.

T   Bike P.M.: 40 miles, rolling hills. Lower cadence to 50 on all uphills.

F   Swim P.M.: 3,600

    6 x 600 (1 = 600 free, 2 = 3 x 200/30 steady, 3 = 600 pull easy, 4 = 6 x 100/20 steady, 5 = 600 free, 6 = 12 x 50 fist drill first 25 on all).

    Run P.M.: 5 miles, easy after swim or separate from swim in A.M.

S   Bike A.M.: 80 miles, steady comfortable ride. Practice race day nutrition on ride.

S   Run A.M.: 16 miles. 30 seconds slower than IM goal first 6 miles. Then IM goal pace final 12 miles.

    Bike P.M.: 15 miles, easy and comfortable, active recovery a few hours after run.

WEEK 13 (BUILD)

M   Swim A.M. or P.M.: 4,000

    1,000 easy and steady. 400 + 4 x 100/30, 300 + 3 x 100/20, 200 + 2 x 100/10. 200 slow pull recovery. 12 x 50 drill 25, free 25. Alternate catch-up and fist drill. 400 easy pull.

T   Run A.M.: 6 miles. Build up to IM goal pace.

    Bike P.M.: 25 miles, steady ride, comfortable pace. Target 50 rpm for all uphills.

W   Swim A.M.: 1,600

    400 pull easy. 20 x 50/10 all brisk, steady. 200 pull easy.

    Run A.M.: 3 miles. Treadmill after swim. IM goal pace, 0% incline.

    Run P.M.: 7 miles. 2 miles slow, then work in 5 x 3 minute

intervals, 5K–10K pace with 2-minute slow jog
between each for recovery. After set, run IM goal pace
to 15 seconds slower to end.

T Swim A.M.: 1,600

Continuous steady swim. Work in 6 x 12 stroke sprints
during the final 800.

Bike P.M.: 40 miles. First 20 miles comfortable and steady.
Then 3 x 10 minute intervals about Olympic–half
Ironman pace with target rpm of 75–80 and higher
gear. 5 minutes easy between each.

F Swim A.M. or P.M.: 4,000

5 x 800/30 (1 = 800 free, with catch-up drill first 25 of each
100, 2 = 4 x 200/30 steady, 3 = 800 pull easy, 4 = 4 x
200/20 steady, 5 = 800 free at comfortable pace).

S Bike A.M.: 90 miles, comfortable pace, rolling hills.
Practice race day nutrition on ride.

Run P.M.: 3 miles. Run slow first 5 minutes then IM goal
pace for the remainder. Keep separate from bike by at
least 3–4 hours.

S Run A.M.: 16 miles, steady run, 30 seconds slower than
goal pace first 4 miles, IM goal pace next 8 miles, 15
seconds faster than goal pace final 4 miles. Practice
race day nutrition.

Bike P.M.: 18 miles, or 50 minutes on trainer. Recovery
spin, slow and relaxed.

WEEK 14 (BUILD)

M Swim A.M.: 3,000

500 pull easy. 40 x 50/10 or on 1-minute cycle, but give at
least 10 seconds rest. All are steady and even pace. 500
pull easy.

T Bike P.M.: 22 miles, comfortable pace, keep all uphills
controlled pace, not too hard.

Run P.M.: 4 miles, brick off bike. 1 mile 30 seconds slower

then IM goal, 2 miles at IM goal, 1 mile at 30 seconds faster than IM goal.

W   Swim A.M.: 2,000

800 easy, do catch-up drill first 25 of each 100. 6 x 100/20 descend 1–3, then repeat descend 4–6. 600 free, steady even pace.

Run P.M.: 7 miles. 2 miles easy, then work in 5 x 3 minutes at 10K pace with 3 minutes between at IM goal pace. After set, run easy to finish.

T   Bike P.M.: 30 miles. 10 miles easy and comfortable. Then work in 2 x 12 minute intervals about half Ironman effort with cadence of 75–80 using higher gear.

F   Run A.M.: 5 miles, slow recovery run. About 1 minute slower than IM goal pace.

Swim P.M.: 3,000

Pyramid with 20-second rest between everything: 100–200–300–400–500–600–500–400–300–200–100. Pace increase second half.

S   Bike A.M.: 100 miles, varied terrain, flat and rolling hills. Don't push hills too hard, but try to control effort by lowering cadence to 50–60 rpm. Practice race day nutrition on ride.

S   Run A.M.: 18 miles. 4 miles 30 seconds slower then IM goal, then run 12 miles at IM goal. Final 2 miles you can maintain or increase to 15–30 seconds faster than IM goal pace if feeling good. Practice race day nutrition on run.

Bike P.M.: 18 miles or 50 minutes on trainer. Recovery pace, very easy.

WEEK 15 (RECOVERY)

M   Day off.

T   Swim A.M.: 3,200.

600 pull easy. 2 x 300/20 descend. 4 x 50/10 kickboard. 6 x 150/20 middle 50. Catch-up drill on the middle 50

yards of all 6 intervals. 12 x 75/30 first 6 sprint first 12 strokes of first 25. Final 6 sprint 12 strokes final 25 of each.

W   Swim P.M.: 2,000

200 easy pull. 4 x 50/10 kickboard. 1,600 continuous steady even pace.

Bike P.M.: 25 miles, easy comfortable ride, very easy on the hills.

T   Run A.M.: 6 miles, easy, no faster than IM goal pace to 30 seconds slower.

Bike P.M.: 45 minutes on trainer. 20 minutes steady. Then 16 x 30 seconds single leg (8 each leg), all at 50 rpm and moderate effort. Go on 1-minute cycles.

F   Day off.

S   Bike A.M.: 60 miles, rolling hills.

Run A.M.: 6 miles, brick off bike. Run 1 mile 30 seconds slower than IM goal pace. Then IM goal pace for 3 miles, 15 seconds faster than goal pace for 2 miles. Practice race day nutrition on bike and run.

S   Run A.M.: 14 miles. 4 miles 15–30 seconds slower than IM goal pace. Then run IM goal pace for remainder if feeling good. No faster.

WEEK 16 (BUILD)

M   Swim A.M. or P.M.: 3,000, continuous steady pace.

T   Run A.M.: 4 miles, easy steady run.

Bike P.M.: 25 miles, steady ride, rolling hills, comfortable pace.

Run P.M.: 3 miles. Brick off bike. 5 minutes 30 seconds slower than IM goal pace, then IM goal pace.

W   Swim A.M.: 2,000

500 pull, easy. 6 x 200/20 descend 1–3, then repeat 4–6. 300 pull, easy.

Run P.M.: 7 miles. 15–30 seconds faster than IM goal, but

work in 1 x 1 minute 5K pace stride per mile.

T   Swim A.M.: 1,600

Continuous swim, steady, even splits.

Run A.M.: 3 miles. Treadmill after swim, IM goal pace at 0% grade.

Bike P.M.: 35 miles. 10 miles easy. Then work in 2 x 15 minute intervals at half Ironman effort with target cadence of 75–80 rpm, higher gear, then easy to end.

F   Swim P.M.: 4,000

5 x 800/30 (1 = 800 free, do catch-up drill first 25 each 100, 2 = 2 x 400/20 descend, 3 = 800 pull slow, 4 = 4 x 200/20 all steady even pace, 5 = 4 x 100/30 descend + 400 free, steady pace.

S   Bike A.M.: 100 miles, mixed terrain, don't push hard on uphills.

S   Run A.M.: 14 miles. Easy run 30 seconds slower than IM goal first 4 miles, then IM goal for the remainder.

WEEK 17 (BUILD)

M   Bike A.M.: 18 miles, 50 minutes on trainer. Steady pace, comfortable.

Swim P.M.: 3,200

3 sets, 1-minute rest between sets (3 x 100/20 descend + 4 x 50/15 descend). Then 800 free, steady even pace.

T   Run A.M.: 5 miles, slow recovery run.

Bike P.M.: 25 miles, steady ride, keep pace easy on hills.

W   Swim A.M.: 2,400

4 x 600/30 descend 1–3, then pull final one easy.

Run P.M.: 7 miles. 2 miles slow, then run IM goal pace and work in 1 x 2 minutes at 10K pace per mile.

T   Bike P.M.: 35 miles. Easy 10 miles, then 3 x 6 minutes Olympic pace intervals choice cadence, 3 minutes easy recovery between each. Steady comfortable pace after.

F   Run A.M.: 6 miles, easy.
    Swim P.M.: 3,500
    1,500 continuous comfortable pace. Then 30 x 50/10 all
        strong and even pace. 500 pull easy.
S   Bike A.M.: 65 miles, steady comfortable ride, rolling hills.
        Target 50 rpm on uphills.
    Run P.M.: 4 miles. 5 minutes at 30 seconds slower than IM
        goal pace, then run IM goal pace.
S   Run A.M.: 18 miles. 2 miles 30 seconds slower than IM goal
        pace. Then IM goal pace for 16 miles.

WEEK 18 (BUILD)

M   Swim P.M.: 4,000
    800 free, catch-up drill first 25 of each 100. 2 x 300/20 even
        and steady.
    3 x 200/30 descend. 4 x 25/10 kickboard recovery. 10 x
        100/20 all strong but even, steady 4 x 25/10 kickboard
        recovery. 12 x 50/10 fist drill first 25, free final 25 on all.
        200 pull slow.
T   Bike A.M.: 20 miles, do 60 minutes on trainer. 30 minutes
        comfortable steady pace. Then 12 x 45 second single
        leg (6 each) at 60 rpm. Start on 1-minute cycles. Easy
        after to end of spin.
W   Swim A.M.: 2,000
    4 x 500/30. First one pull, final three descend slightly.
    Run P.M.: 8 miles. Steady run after few minutes slow, run
        IM goal pace to 15 seconds faster.
T   Run A.M.: 4 miles easy slow, about 30 seconds slower than
        IM goal pace.
    Bike P.M.: 40 miles. 20 miles comfortable pace. Then do 20
        minutes at Olympic to half Ironman pace with target
        cadence of 75–80 rpm using bigger gear. After, ride
        easy to end.
F   Swim A.M. or P.M.: 4,000

2,000 continuous. Then 30 x 50/10 all steady and even pace. 500 pull slow.

S   Bike A.M.: 60 miles, steady comfortable pace, rolling hills. Keep uphill effort controlled by lowering cadence to 50 rpm.

Run A.M.: 6 miles, brick off bike. Run 1 mile 30 seconds slower than IM goal pace. Then run IM goal pace next mile. Final 4 miles, run 30 seconds faster than goal pace if comfortable.

S   Run A.M.: 18 miles. 12 miles at or down to 30 seconds slower than IM goal pace. Final 6 miles can increase pace if feeling good up to 30 seconds faster than IM goal pace but no faster.

WEEK 19 (RECOVERY)

M   Day off.

T   Swim P.M.: 2,800

600 free easy. 4 x 50/10 kickboard. 8 x 200/30 all steady pace, even. 400 pull easy.

Run P.M.: 4 miles, easy after swim. IM goal pace at 0% grade.

W   Run A.M.: 5 miles, easy recovery pace.

Bike P.M.: 25 miles, easy comfortable ride, very easy on the hills.

T   Swim A.M.: 2,000

Continuous swim, easy and steady.

Bike P.M.: 25 miles. 10 miles easy. Then 20 minutes half Ironman pace at 75 rpm. 10 minutes easy. Then 10 minutes Olympic tri pace at 80–85 rpm. 5 minutes easy. Then 5 minutes sprint tri pace at 90–95 rpm.

F   Day off.

S   Swim A.M.: 2,200

400 pull easy. 6 x 150/20 middle 50 on first 3 catch-up drill,

middle 50 on final 3 is fist drill. 400 pull easy. 500 free tempo but even pace.

Bike A.M.: 60 miles, rolling hills. Keep cadence at 50 on uphills.

S   Run A.M.: 14 miles. 4 miles 15–30 seconds slower than IM goal pace. Then can run IM goal pace remainder of run if feeling good. No faster.

WEEK 20 (BUILD)

M   Swim A.M.: 3,000

500 pull easy. 40 x 50/10 all steady and even pace. 500 pull slow.

Run P.M.: 5 miles, easy recovery run.

T   Bike P.M.: 22 miles, steady comfortable pace on rolling hills. On all uphills keep cadence at 50.

Run P.M.: 4 miles brick off bike. 5 minutes 30 seconds slower than IM goal pace, then run IM goal pace.

W   Swim A.M.: 2,000

800 free, steady even pace. 3 x 200/30 descend, 4 x 100/30 descend. 200 pull.

Run A.M.: 3 miles. Treadmill after swim. IM goal pace at 0% grade for 1 mile. 30 seconds faster than IM goal pace next 2 miles.

Run P.M.: 7 miles. 2 miles slow. Final 5 miles, run first 3 minutes of each mile at 5K–10K pace, then remainder of mile at 30 seconds slower than IM goal pace (5 x 3 minute intervals).

T   Swim A.M.: 1,600

Continuous swim, steady and even pace.

Bike P.M.: 40 miles. 20 miles comfortable, then 30-minute intervals at half Ironman pace, but target cadence is 75 and higher gear. Ride easy to end.

F   Swim P.M.: 4,000

    4 x 1,000/45, stretch during 45-second rest (1 = 1,000 free, steady even pace, 2 = 5 x 200/20 all, even pace, 3 = 1,000 pull, slow easy, 4 = 5 x 100/20 strong but even pace + 500 free, steady even pace).

S   Bike A.M.: 90 miles, mixed terrain, rolling hills. Keep pace comfortable.

S   Run A.M.: 18 miles. First 2 miles 30 seconds slower than IM goal pace. Next 12 at IM goal pace. Final 4 maintain or can run 15–30 seconds faster than goal pace if feeling good.

WEEK 21 (BUILD)

M   Swim A.M.: 3,000

    5 x 600/30 (1 = 600 free with catch-up drill first 25 each 100, 2 = 3 x 200/20 descend, 3 = 600 pull, slow, 4 = 12 x 50/15 first 6 sprint 12 strokes first 25, final 6 sprint 12 strokes final 25, 5 = 600 free, steady even pace).

    Bike P.M.: 18 miles, easy recovery ride.

T   Bike P.M.: 25 miles, steady pace on rolling hills. Keep cadence at 50 on uphills.

W   Swim A.M.: 2,000

    1,500 steady even pace continuous. 10 x 50/10 all strong but even pace.

    Run P.M.: 8 miles. 2 miles easy, slow. Then run first 1 minute of each mile at 5K pace and remainder of each mile at IM goal pace.

T   Run A.M.: 4 miles, easy recovery pace.

    Bike P.M.: 35 miles, steady ride, rolling hills, cadence 50 on uphills.

F   Swim P.M.: 4,000

    5 x 800/30 (1 = 800 free, do catch-up drill first 25 each 100,

2 = 2 x 400/20 descend, 3 = 800 pull, slow, 4 = 4 x
200/20 all, steady even pace, 5 = 4 x 100/30 descend +
400 free, steady pace.

S Bike A.M.: 80 miles, keep pace comfortable, practice race
day nutrition.

S Run A.M.: 18 miles. First 4 miles 30 seconds slower than
IM goal pace. Then 14 miles at IM goal pace.

WEEK 22 (BUILD)

M Swim A.M.: 3,200

1,500 continuous steady even pace. 4 x 50/10 kickboard
recovery. 8 x 100/20 all are strong but even pace. 10 x
50/15, each set of 5, drop 1 breath per stroke (breathe
every 2nd/3rd/4th/5th/6th stroke) then repeat. Key is to
focus on slowing down on longer breath holds and
focus on long complete strokes. 200 pull easy.

Bike P.M.: 15 miles or 45 minutes on trainer. 15 minutes
easy. Then 2 x 1 minute hard intervals at 100 rpm with
2 minutes easy recovery between. At 20 minutes do 3 x
5 minute intervals all at Olympic-sprint tri effort, but
target is 75–80 rpm and higher gear. 2 minutes
recovery between each.

T Bike A.M. or P.M.: 21 miles, steady comfortable ride on
rolling hills. Keep cadence at 50 on uphills.

Run A.M. or P.M.: 3 miles brick off bike. 5 minutes at easy
pace 30 seconds slower than IM goal, then remainder
of run is at 30 seconds faster than IM goal pace.

W Swim A.M.: 3,000

Pyramid: 500 free + 5 x 100/30, 400 free + 4 x 100/20, 300
free + 3 x 100/10, 200 free + 2 x 100/5. 200 easy pull.
On all that are "free" the pace is comfortable, and all
100s are brisk.

Run P.M.: 6 miles. Base pace is 15–30 seconds slower than IM goal. Every 4 minutes base pace, run 1 minute at 5K pace for entire run.

T   Run A.M.: 4 miles, recovery run, easy pace.

Bike P.M.: 35 miles. First 15 miles comfortable pace. Then do 2 x 15 minute intervals at Olympic tri pace, but target cadence is 75. 5 minutes easy recovery between intervals. Easy pace after to end.

F   Swim A.M. or P.M.: 3,200

4 x 800/30 (1 = 800 free, catch-up drill first 25 of each 100, 2 = 4 x 200/20 tempo and even pace, 3 = 800 free, steady even pace, 4 = 4 x 100/20 all hard + 400 free, steady even pace).

S   Bike A.M.: 50 miles

Steady comfortable pace 20 miles. Then 30-minute interval at half Ironman pace and effort at target cadence of 75 using higher gear. 5 minutes slow recovery pace. Then 15 minutes at Olympic tri pace with target cadence of 80. 5 minutes slow recovery pace. Then 5 minutes at sprint tri pace (controlled, not "all out") with target cadence of 85. After set, ride comfortable pace to end.

Run A.M.: 10 miles.

Brick off bike. Run miles 1–2 at 30 seconds slower than IM goal pace. Miles 3–4 at 15 seconds slower than IM goal pace, miles 5–7 at IM goal pace, miles 8–10 at 15–30 seconds faster than IM goal pace. Practice race day nutrition on both bike and run.

S   Day off.

WEEK 23 (PRETAPER)

M   Swim A.M.: 3,000

2,000 continuous, steady even pace. 4 x 25/10 kickboard

recovery. 12 x 50/15 each set of 6, drop 1 breath per stroke (breathe every 2nd/3rd/4th/5th/6th/7th stroke), then repeat. Key is to focus on slowing down on longer breath holds and focus on long complete strokes to lower heart rate.

T   Run A.M. or P.M.: 4 miles, easy steady pace, average pace is IM goal pace.

W   Bike P.M.: 40 miles.

Comfortable pace for 15 miles, easy. Then do 3 x 6 minute intervals at half Ironman goal pace, but target is 75 rpm and higher gear. 2 minutes easy recovery spin between. After interval set, ride easy and comfortable to end.

T   Run P.M.: 18 miles.

4 miles 15–30 seconds slower than IM goal pace. Then 10 miles at IM goal pace. Final 4 miles maintain, or if feeling good can run 15–30 seconds faster than IM goal pace.

F   Swim P.M.: 4,000.

4 x 1,000/30 (1 = 1,000 free, steady even pace, 2 = 2 x 500/20 steady but descend, 3 = 5 x 200/15 all steady even pace, 4 = 5 x 100/20 sprint 12 strokes during first 25 of each, then slow down to steady even pace. After 5 x 100, swim 500 free at same pace as first 1,000).

S   Bike A.M.: 60 miles, easy pace entire ride. Can ride rolling hills, but do not push the hills hard.

S   Run A.M.: 12 miles.

Easy pace 15–30 seconds slower than IM goal pace. Final 4 miles do 1 x 45-second pick up to about 10K pace per mile.

WEEK 24 (TAPER)

M Swim A.M. or P.M.: 3,000 or 1 hour, continuous easy and
      even pace.

T   Run A.M.: 4 miles.
      Pace is easy, 30 seconds slower than IM goal pace. Final 2
        miles work in 4 x 30 second strides at 5K pace (not
        sprinting), with 2 minutes easy pace between.
      Bike P.M.: 23 miles.
      Easy comfortable pace. After 30 minutes work in 3 x 2
        minute intervals at Olympic tri pace, but increase
        cadence on each from 75 to 85 to 95 on final interval. 4
        minutes easy recovery between each. Ride comfortable
        after set to end.

W Day off.

T   Swim A.M.: 1,600
      400 pull easy. 4 x 100/30 sprint first 12 strokes on all, then
        remainder of 100 is easy. 400 pull easy. 8 x 50/15
        catch-up drill first 25, strong pace second 25 on all.
      Bike A.M. or P.M.: 18 miles.
      Easy comfortable pace. After 30 minutes work in 3 x 1
        minute intervals like Tuesday's ride. 2 minutes easy
        recovery pace between each.

F   Day off.

S   Bike A.M.: 30 minutes easy with 3 x 30 second intervals at
        100 rpm to loosen legs up, 2 minutes easy recovery
        between each.
      Run A.M.: 15 minutes.
      Brick off bike. Run recovery pace, and work in 3 x 20
        second strides at 5K pace just to loosen legs up. 2
        minutes easy recovery pace between intervals.

S   *RACE*

The Never Stop Foundation

"Never Stop" is the motto of my life, and in 2007 I named my foundation after it. The Never Stop Foundation is dedicated to using athletics as a tool to give underserved youths the chance to achieve their full potential. The foundation's mission is to find and build the Never Stop Performance Center in Kailua-Kona, Hawaii, beginning in 2011. The center will be a training and learning facility to help children and adults discover and achieve their God-given potential through fitness, athletic training, sports, and community.

If you would like to find out more about supporting the Never Stop Foundation with donations, expertise, or ideas, please visit www.neverstopfoundation.org.

Acknowledgments

I'm grateful to so many for helping me create the life I have today:

- To my heavenly father, I'm both honored and humbled that you have chosen to use me as your vessel to reach the world, one soul at a time.

- To my precious daughter, Katana, there isn't a minute that goes by that I don't think of you. You're the biggest inspiration in my life. I love you and give you to the Lord as my gift. Thank you for inspiring me to be the best. You're in good hands.

- To my dad, thank you for being my best friend and biggest inspiration.

- To my mother, whom I never had the chance to know, thank you for bringing me into this world.

- To my grandmother, to whom I feel deeply indebted, you took me in at an early age as one of your own. We both lost the loves of our lives, and we weathered the storm together. I now understand that the Lord sent you to be my angel. Thank you for sticking by my side as my prayer warrior.

- To the entire Lester, Uzzanto, Randolph, and Williams families, thank you.

- To my agent, Jillian Manus, thank you for listening to God's calling on this project. I told you from day one that you are an angel sent to me. I'm forever indebted to you. Thank you for standing by my side and helping me bring this book to fruition.

- To Theresa Van Eeghen and the whole staff at Manus and Associates for your hard work to ensure this project was the best it could be.

- To my coauthor, Tim Vandehey, you made me feel like family from day one. If it weren't for you, I would have never shared these words. I'm excited about this project but more excited about our future together as friends.

- I thank Rip Oldmeadow for listening to the Lord.

- To Maria Schulman, Cynthia DiTiberio, Suzanne Quist, Julie Burton, Jamie Brickhouse, Michele Wetherbee, and everyone at HarperOne—thank you for being a blessed part of my journey.

- To my Ultraman family, thank you for all your love and support as well as being some of my biggest inspirations.

- To my friend and mentor, Rich Roll, our spiritual connection is by far one of the most positive forces in my life. Thank you for bringing the best out of me on and off the course. The journey has just begun!

- To my half brother, Quinton, for taking me under your broken wing at the tender age of five and watching me when we were both lost, you're an angel and you don't even know it . . . yet.

- To Nathan LaDuke, you were my role model starting at age nine. Not just for your athletic ability, but as a man of God. Thank you.

- To my coaches who helped mold me at an early age to be the best athlete I could possibly be: Coach Marfe for showing me what an Ironman triathlete was when I was fourteen; also to John Cadenhead, Art Misuraca, Coach Lautt, and Coach Nevins.

- To the Kelhoffer family: Chuck, Diane, Billy, Chad, and Karen. Chuck, you were one of my biggest inspirations as a child and still are twenty years later. God used you to protect me back then, and you've still got my back.

- To Harold Chapple, I love you. Thank you for being you, my brother in Christ and my prayer warrior.

- To Harlan Werner; Tom Loeffler; the Klitschko brothers, Vladimir and Vitali; Muhammad Ali; and Stephen Holland, words can't describe the respect and gratitude I have for you all. Thank you for showing me that anything is possible.

- To my friend, mentor, and coach Dave Ciaverella: as you know, I'm not one for words. I'm an actions kind of guy. Thank you for believing in my mission, journey, and message. I'm blessed to have you in my life.

- To my friends: Mike Brown, Steve Claiborne, Fred Hunt, Jason Woodburn, Jay Cadenhead, Jerry Hahn, Matty Cunningham, Pat Cunningham, Richard and Patty, Doug and Annette, Jane Bockus, Steve Brown, Steve King, Dean Karnazes, Cory Foulk, Karlyn Pipes-Neilsen, and Eric Neilsen. You all inspire me and keep me going.

- To all my sponsors: ZOOT Sports—Brian, Jake, Aaron, and Brant—for supporting my journey; to Compton at Ascended Health, you're an angel; Specialized Bikes; the whole crew at Tropical Café Kona; the whole gang at BikeWorks for being all class and VIP treatment; the Vitamin Shoppe; and James Gilbert.

- Special thanks go out to my angels: Vivian, Rebecca, Kellie, David, Lincoln, Stan, and the hundreds of friends on my social networks who e-mail and call with encouragement. Without your support, none of this would be possible.

- And for the thousands who voted for me for the 2009 ESPY Award, I know who you are. You're on my team—and we are all an inspiration. We all have a story, and I'll forever be indebted to you for your faith in me.